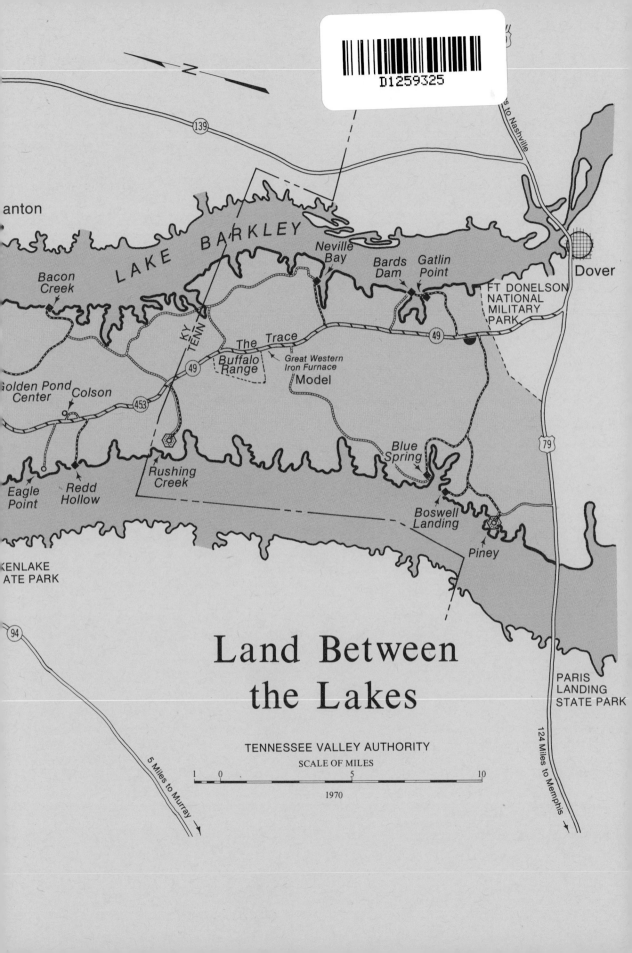

Land Between the Lakes

TENNESSEE VALLEY AUTHORITY

SCALE OF MILES

1970

Map labels:

139

anton

LAKE BARKLEY

Bacon Creek

Neville Bay

Bards Dam

Gatlin Point

Dover

FT DONELSON NATIONAL MILITARY PARK

to Nashville

KY
TENN

The Trace

Buffalo Range

Great Western Iron Furnace

Model

49

Golden Pond Center

Colson

453

Blue Spring

79

Eagle Point

Redd Hollow

Rushing Creek

Boswell Landing

Piney

KENLAKE
ATE PARK

94

5 Miles to Murray

PARIS LANDING STATE PARK

124 Miles to Memphis

Land Between the Lakes

Land Between the Lakes

Experiment in Recreation

by Frank E. Smith

Introduction by Roderick Nash

The University Press of Kentucky

Standard Book Number 8131-1242-7

Library of Congress Catalog Card Number 71-132831

COPYRIGHT © 1971 BY THE UNIVERSITY PRESS OF KENTUCKY

A statewide cooperative scholarly publishing agency serving Berea College, Centre College of Kentucky, Eastern Kentucky University, Kentucky State College, Morehead State University, Murray State University, University of Kentucky, University of Louisville, and Western Kentucky University.

Editorial and Sales Offices: Lexington, Kentucky 40506

Contents

Introduction by Roderick Nash

If a large snake crawled in front of you right now—right as you read these words—your reaction would almost certainly be one of instinctive terror and hostility. You would scream, run, look for a stick, pick up a rock—probably all at the same time. And you would be in good company. Most Americans suffer from an environmental bias that makes snakes objects of fear rather than of wonder and curiosity. The hatred of snakes, and the list might well be expanded to include spiders, hawks, wolves, and skunks, has two main sources. One stems from an overdose of urban civilization, the other from the hangover of frontier-bred utilitarianism.

The most profound significance of the Land Between the Lakes Recreation Area is that it constitutes an imaginative, aggressive effort to overcome the environmental blindness that engenders, for one thing, hatred of snakes. Indeed, after a week in this magic almost-island, you would probably delight in the appearance of a snake—you might even know its name!

At first glance environmental education, such as Land Between the Lakes offers, seems to have little direct relevance to the much-publicized environmental crisis. What takes place in this relatively small area seems to have no bearing on the nightmarish problems of pollution facing our civilization. Exposing people to nature, one might argue, is an amenity—it's nice but irrelevant to the ultimate concern of survival. Land Between the Lakes, according to this viewpoint, is a hold-over from the cosmetic-like conservation of a decade ago. So the question of Land Between the Lakes's legitimacy naturally arises. Wouldn't the Tennessee Valley Authority better use its dollars and energy to attack environmental challenges like cleaning the air, purifying the water, and defusing the population bomb? Isn't creating Land Between the Lakes much like refurnishing a schoolhouse and play area that lies squarely in the path of a rapidly advancing tornado?

Reflection exposes the fallacy of this line of reasoning and the transcendent wisdom of Frank Smith and his colleagues in the creation of Land Between the Lakes. Such undertakings, in fact, ultimately hold the key to stopping the approaching menace of environmental deterioration. The analogy of the schoolhouse was somewhat mis-conceived. A real tornado is entirely natural. Man neither causes it nor finds himself in a position to stop its effects. But the tornado inherent in abuse of the environment is almost entirely man-made. *We* have ushered in the environmental crisis through careless wielding of technological power, and we constitute the last best hope for usher-ing it out. If a new day of environmental peace is to dawn, it will be a *pax homines*—created and maintained by man.

Prerequisite to such a peace, however, is a revolution in our think-ing about man's relationship to the environment. For the future (if there is to be one for life on earth) we need a brand new intellectual wardrobe. Our values, ethics, and priorities must change. We need humility. We need to rediscover a long-lost sense of our limitations and of our consequent dependency on the fragile and beautiful skein of interrelationships called the ecosphere. We must regain a sense of respect for and community with the other life-forms sharing the en-vironment. We cannot live without them. They will not live if sub-jected to our continuing abuse. We must, in sum, develop a profound sense of reverence for our spaceship—the earth. It is the only home we have.

The discovery of truths such as these are almost impossible to make in the condition of overcivilization we occupy today. Aldo Leopold, the pioneer ecologist, realized this when he wrote that "civilization has so cluttered [the] elemental man-earth relation with gadgets and middlemen that awareness of it is growing dim. We fancy that in-dustry supports us, forgetting what supports industry." This was thirty years ago. Today we find it still harder to remember that water doesn't come from the tap, nor heat from the furnace, nor light from a bulb, nor meat neatly wrapped in cellophane from your friendly butcher. To gain a true perspective, and to give it to our children, we desperately need the kind of experience that Land Between the Lakes makes so easy and so enjoyable to obtain.

The best insurance against destruction of the environment, Frank Smith declares, is "full comprehension of nature in an outdoor expo-sure." *Comprehension* is the key word. To their credit the planners of Land Between the Lakes understood that simply chalking up hours outdoors is insufficient. A logger, for example, may have lived his entire life in the woods and still rape the land with his cut-out-and-get-out ethics. And many self-styled sportsmen spend hundreds of hours a year hunting and fishing without acquiring even the simple standards of environmental decency. For this reason Land Between the Lakes goes beyond the mere provision of play space. The underlying philosophy of the project is educational. By exposing people to a healthy environment in such a way that they come to understand and appreciate its intricate balances, Land Between the Lakes builds environmental responsibility.

The significance of this kind of endeavor is heightened when we see it in the light of the history of man's relationship to nature. In the beginning, of course, there was no problem. The precursors of man were part of nature and took their place in it with little or no disruption. But at some point in the dim past a nameless ape, brighter than his fellows, fancied himself superior to other life-forms and aspired to their conquest and domination. As man developed as a species, his ego thrived on the idea that, while not quite an angel, he was still not an animal—not part of nature. This curious belief was written into the Bible. Genesis 1:28 supposes God to have directed man to "be fruitful, and multiply, and replenish the earth and subdue it: and have dominion over the fish of the sea, and over the fowl of the air, and over every living thing that moveth upon the earth." The tragedy here lay in forgetting that man is a member in, not the master of, the environment and that his welfare depends on the welfare of the whole.

The discovery and settlement of the New World accelerated myopic, selfish, and ultimately suicidal ideas about man's place in nature. The frontier spawned the myth of inexhaustibility. There was always a next ridge, another herd of buffalo, more passenger pigeons. The thought of limits on human action with respect to the environment was repugnant to rugged individuals engaged in a race for profits. As a frontiersman, the American instinctively defined progress in terms of growth and development. Nature had to be conquered, the wilderness redeemed for civilization. Coupled with chronic carelessness, this obsession with development entailed environmental deterioration. The root problem was that in regard to the nonhuman world, man had no system of ethics to temper his lusts. For a time damage was limited by the available tools. Axes and shovels only scratched the North American wilderness. But technological progress produced chain saws and bulldozers. New-style pioneers, dignified with the title of captains of industry, used them to cut deeper. The land proved astonishingly resilient, but man's capacity to alter the environment knew no bounds. An end, of a sort, was reached in the summer of 1945 when the United States unveiled a super tool—the atomic bomb. The prospect of environmental annihilation was now very real. Man had indeed secured dominion "over every living thing that moveth upon the earth."

Hope in an otherwise grim situation lies in the possibility that the same intelligence threatening the environment can now be enlisted in the tasks of repair and protection. United States history offers some encouragement in this respect. Even as most Americans plunged into the business of environmental exploitation, a few struggled against the current. One thinks of George Catlin, who fathered the national park idea in 1832; Henry David Thoreau, who stated that "in Wildness is the preservation of the World"; George Perkins Marsh, whose 1864 concept of "geographical regeneration" was a harbinger of regional planning efforts such as that involving the Tennessee Valley; John Muir, who founded the Sierra Club in 1892. These conservation pioneers, and a handful of others, dared to be different. They had in common a willingness to challenge the dominant conception of the land's purpose and to expose inexhaustibility as a myth. They were also willing to question the dogma of free enterprise which balked at the prospect of government regulation in the interest of the environment. These prophets even dared to suggest that growth and quantity were not the only possible criteria for progress and happiness. The *kind* of life lived amid abundance, they implied, also had its claims and sometimes, as in the case of parks, demanded that limits be set to civilization's expansion.

American conservation first became a "movement" in the Progressive period of the early twentieth century. Americans in these years were ready to be concerned about their environment. A national mood existed that had been absent a generation before. Its primary characteristic was anxiety over change. Industrialization, urbanization, and the growth of population were remaking the country. The frontier had been pronounced dead by the Census of 1890, and a vague uneasiness permeated American culture. The frontier had been almost synon-

ymous with the abundance, opportunity, and distinctiveness of the
New World for two and a half centuries. Few, as a consequence,
could regard its passing without at least a pang of regret. Few could
help wondering whether nature would have much of a role in the
nation of the future.

Progressive conservation took shape in the minds of men like
Gifford Pinchot, Theodore Roosevelt, and philosophers of watershed
management like John Wesley Powell, W J McGee, and Frederick H.
Newell. They shared a determination to manage natural resources
according to scientific principles and in the name of the society as a
whole. But close examination reveals the Progressive conservationists
to be little more than efficient pioneers. Transformation and exploitation of nature remained the dominant concern although now it was
undertaken with careful, farsighted planning. Pinchot, for example,
was devoted to making the nation's forests continually productive. He
regarded forestry as a form of agriculture and proposed to manage
trees as a huge crop. The emphasis was still on conquest and economics.

For the seeds of a different attitude it is necessary to look to the
national park movement. Beginning with the creation of Yellowstone
National Park in 1872, the United States opened a new chapter in
environmental history. Our national parks were novel in that they
preserved unmodified nature for enjoyment, education, and inspiration. The parks, in other words, celebrated an undisturbed environment rather than one that man had transformed. Implicit here was
an attitude of humility, respect, even of reverence for nature. Americans can be proud of belonging to a civilization that invented national
parks. They are one of our most original and important contributions
to the human endeavor.

The creation of the Tennessee Valley Authority in 1933 marked
another milestone in the emergence of an American land ethic. David
Lilienthal, one of the initial directors of TVA, recognized the larger
significances of the undertaking. "For the first time since the trees
fell before the settlers' ax," he wrote, "America set out to command
nature not by defying her, as in that wasteful past, but by understanding and acting upon her first law—the oneness of man and natural
resources, the unity that binds together land, streams, forests, minerals,
and mankind." With TVA multipurpose development of an entire
watershed, a dream of conservationists since the turn of the century,
became a reality. The people in the valley stood to benefit, but so

did the valley itself. Progress, that is to say, was to come in connection with, rather than at the expense of, the environment as a whole. TVA thus repudiated the old exploitative philosophy and became an international byword for regional planning. Here, too, was an American contribution to world civilization.

In the two decades following the Second World War, the driving force in the American conservation movement came increasingly from the quest for quality in the environment. Many Americans have come to understand that an environment conducive to survival—even to affluence—was not enough. The land, they insisted, had to do more than just keep people alive—it had to bring them joy. Beautification, for example, became a primary conservation goal of the early 1960s.

In the very recent past, however, the emphasis swung back to survival. Scared by catastrophes such as smog over major cities, an oil spill in the Santa Barbara Channel, and the ending of Lake Erie's capacity to support life, the public woke up to the fact of environmental deterioration. "Environment" filled the nation's publications and the minds of its citizens. Ecologists finally had their day in the national spotlight. Americans began to understand the implications for their own lives, of John Muir's maxim that "when you try to pick out anything by itself, you find it hitched to everything in the universe." Mere beautification no longer satisfied. Many regarded this kind of conservation as cosmetic, aimed at covering rather than curing environmental ills. The real problem, it became apparent, was man. Environmentalists widely quoted Pogo to the effect that "we have met the enemy and he is us." Our tastes and values, our life-styles, our exorbitant demand for goods and for energy, our wastefulness—the whole polluted chain of thinking that led man to regard the world as his private object of exploitation—this was the basic enemy in the battle for survival.

If *mind* pollution is the basic problem, then environmental education, leading to ecological awareness, is the essential antidote. Land Between the Lakes stands as one of its most imaginative applications. It should be seen as part of the growing emphasis on ecology that is already transforming the curricula of schools and colleges. Land Between the Lakes injects a sorely needed transfusion of encouragement into the environmental movement. It proves that in at least a small portion of the earth man can return to sanity.

Preface

THIS BOOK has been prepared in response to a number of requests for a history of the Land Between the Lakes recreational area and the development of the project by the Tennessee Valley Authority (TVA). Both the history of the area itself and the planning and development of the recreation project and program are outlined here. The viewpoint, naturally, is that of the people responsible for the planning and carrying forward of the Land Between the Lakes demonstration—the staff and directors of the Tennessee Valley Authority.

Land Between the Lakes is a significant experiment in the transformation of submarginal land—enhanced in this instance by the addition of reservoir shoreline—into a large-scale, multiple-use recreational facility. It can serve well as a demonstration model for future developments, of similar scope, both in the United States and in other parts of the world. The orientation of Land Between the Lakes to conservation education gives this demonstration special importance in a period when the pressures of population and urban living have added a new dimension to the significance of conservation.

It is my hope that this book will increase the impact of the Land Between the Lakes demonstration in creating an awareness of the demands and importance of the new conservation. If that objective is achieved, it will constitute a bonus to the book's more pedestrian values. These include the planning of related type nature-based recreation facilities and the provision of background information for both regular and casual visitors to Land Between the Lakes.

The book itself is the product of a collaborative effort with many members of the TVA staff. I would like to express special appreciation to the staff of Land Between the Lakes; to the TVA information staff; and to my secretary, Mrs. Mary F. Knurr. Research by Dr. J. Milton Henry of Austin Peay State University was of great value in preparation of the section on the historical background of the land between the rivers region.

TVA has great hopes that Land Between the Lakes will rank as one of the agency's major contributions to improvement of the quality of American life.

The pictures of reptiles, amphibians, wildflowers, ferns, and lichens in this book are the work of the Biology Department of Austin Peay State University, Clarksville, Tennessee. They were taken in Land Between the Lakes under a contract with the Tennessee Valley Authority. Many of the photographs of birds and other wildlife are the work of Karl Maslowski, nationally known wildlife lecturer and photographer from Cincinnati, Ohio.

FRANK E. SMITH

Land Between the Lakes

Chapter One

Space for All the People

AMERICA NEEDS more open space and open air for the recreation needs of its growing population. The varieties of space needed range from vest-pocket, quarter-acre green swards in the cities to vast wilderness areas in the mountains. The vest-pockets can be built on the site of condemned, deserted buildings, and upon occasion the land may be donated by public-spirited individuals or business firms. Most of the space, however, will have to be bought and paid for by some level of government. Quite often—and more often in the future than in the past—the process will require purchase by condemnation.

During the past ten years the major success in the nation in acquiring open space for public recreation has been the conception and development by the Tennessee Valley Authority of the Land Between the Lakes recreation area in western Kentucky and Tennessee. The TVA demonstration in conservation-based recreation provides no panacea for the national need or automatic solutions for the multiplicity of problems connected with it, but it does make clear some obvious lessons that can be of value in meeting the open space needs of the nation in the years immediately ahead.

In summary, a number of ingredients contributed significantly to the effectiveness of TVA's efforts to acquire and develop the Land Between the Lakes area for public recreation. In varying degrees these ingredients may be applicable to the efforts of others.

First was the assignment of sole responsibility for the entire project —from preliminary planning to physical development—to a single agency. This responsibility was reflected in a firm policy decision, based on competent technical recommendations, on the area to be acquired and a determination that there would be no inholdings or exceptions for the sake of expediency. An integral part of this policy decision was a commitment to defend and sustain this position, both administratively and technically.

A combination of adequate, though limited, annual appropriations and administrative flexibility in dividing the funds available each year between land acquisition and construction of public use facilities made possible a continuing and expanding program. Thus it was possible to be responsive to the interests of the users of the area and those whose land was being purchased. This, in turn, helped build and sustain the essential broad base of public support in the area for the project. Though there was sharp and vociferous opposition, support for the project and confidence in TVA's ability to carry it out fairly and wisely prevailed.

Even with these favorable circumstances, however, many difficult problems were encountered, as they will be encountered in similar efforts elsewhere. But such problems are small in comparison with the overwhelming need to acquire, protect, and preserve open space for the American people. The combinations of population masses with the miseries and savagery of the ghetto and the chaos of urban sprawl require more than patchwork solutions, but no one can deny that an essential part of any solution is to provide more open space so that all Americans will have the opportunity to breathe and relax under open skies.

The case for recreation areas as distinguished from traditional national parks, national forests, and wilderness areas, as well as their counterparts provided by state and local governments, had been made principally by the masses of people who have flocked in vast numbers to use the limited sites and facilities. It has been made also by scholars and students of the overall issue of improving the quality of the environment by better conservation of the basic natural resources.

More than anything else, however, the need for open-space recreational land is made clear by the struggles of every unit of government to meet demands for recreational facilities and areas. Very few, however, are achieving spectacular progress in keeping alive the American ethic that exposure to nature and the outdoors is good for human beings. The outdoors is being fenced in and paved over at a greater rate than the population growth, and there is no longer even the possibility of the old unplanned use of the vacant lot and the farm pasture and woodland, idyllic even including the remote fears of the angry bull.

2

Most of the national parks and the still uncertain wilderness areas were made possible by the happenstance of vast acreages of public lands in the hands of the federal government and comparatively little pressure for their private development. (A large proportion of state and local parks in the country as a whole originated on land made available by federal largesse and occasional private benevolence.) In the years after World War II the federal government, with much rhetoric from both the administrative and legislative branches, adopted a policy of federal acquisition of privately owned lands to provide new parks and recreational areas, especially in locations accessible to large masses of population. (The very origin of most of the early parks made them inaccessible to most of the nation, and even in today's travel patterns their accessibility is primarily to the most affluent portion of the population.) Despite the changed policy, however, no major authorizations were made until 1961.

New national parks were authorized with great flourishes and high hopes. Acquisition of the necessary land and development of facilities would be dependent upon later appropriations, as part of the overall budget of the Department of the Interior. Competing with war, space, health, poverty, pollution, and all the other demands on the federal budget, and always with steadily rising prices, park development has not fared well.

Today, however, an involved, informed, and sophisticated public is unwilling to accept the idea that national parks are distant, once-in-a-lifetime trips, part of expensive vacationlands available only to the most affluent. The general affluence and the interstate highway system have made the parks of the West part of the regular travel program of a great segment of middle-income America. Still, the great majority of the visitors are drawn from the top side of our economic dividing lines. Cost and distance make it impossible for the economically less fortunate to make extensive use of the facilities.

The younger segment of our population, whether the young family that is the chief user of outdoor recreation facilities or the unattached college-age young, is not only directly involved in the push for more public facilities but also showing far greater concern for the availability of facilities for the low-income groups of the cities. For most of the urban poor, one of their greatest needs is clean open space close to home. Enough remains, however, of the emotional appeal for the traditional joys and merits of hiking and fishing, hunting and camping to make their needs and demands for land and water more than is available in even the best urban park systems.

The frontier concept of limitless resources available for exploitation and waste is often blamed for many of the current perils to the American environment. Open space recreation, with emphasis upon camping and outdoor life related to conservation education and firmly fixed conservation rules, is an obvious way to bridge the gap between the sometimes-mythical frontier heritage and the necessity for more conservation of resources.

The young people involved in providing leadership for the new concern with quality environment are not going to accept the elitist conservation concept which has prevailed too often in national park development concepts—that the open spaces must be preserved primarily for those endowed with a capacity to appreciate fully the joys and beauty of nature, and protected from the hordes of ordinary Americans who might overrun them. The one way to preserve some semblance of nature undefiled in some spots is to make far more open space available to great masses of the people on an active or at least a semi-participatory basis, even if the participation is no more than limited hikes.

The problems of acquiring and preserving land for open space recreation are going to become more difficult with each passing year. Decisions must be made to meet the rising costs and to face up fully to the unpleasant fact that adequate areas are not going to be secured on a voluntary, step-by-step basis. Land costs have been generally outpacing the overall rate of inflation in the past few years. The very factors which dictate the need for more public acquisition and development of open land—the growing population on a more congested landscape—are what make the land more valuable. In our more affluent society there are very few landowners who do not feel that they can always wait for a higher price.

One small way to alleviate the problem will come through organizations like the National Park Foundation, chartered by Congress to accept private (tax-deductible) gifts to "preserve the nation's natural, historic and recreational resources." The idea is that private money can purchase land for new park sites before they are actually authorized and thereby establish a fair market value for land before speculation enters the picture. The scheme will be of unquestioned value, but it would be unrealistic optimism to expect major benefits.

First of all, there has been no great rush of private wealth to endow the Foundation. Many millions would be needed to get a revolving fund sufficient to meet a reasonable proportion of the demands over the country. There is also no assurance that courts and juries will attach greater validity to property transactions involving the Foundation than they will to the history of other unrelated private transactions. There is an old tradition, old enough to be called an "old American" tradition, that any unit of government is fair game in respect to the unwilling sale of private property to government. Eminent domain is an essential power in the purchase of property by government, and so is review of this authority by the courts, but the general public seems to accept the idea that government should be charged a high price. The widow with the shotgun defending the old homestead against heartless big government is a stereotype of journalistic news value that never seems to lose its appeal, no matter what the purpose of the proposed land acquisition. Much of the present-day reaction against "the establishment" automatically accepts the worth of any claim against the government, and this judgment often carries over against the social purpose of the government project involved.

This immediately adds up to a basic contradiction between the pressures for open space and the support for implementing open space programs, which, in turn, illuminates the essential failure fully to inform the public. As with all conservation and environmental quality projects and programs, the cost and the problems of acquiring land must be admitted from the start and accepted as part of the price which must be paid to achieve the desired ends. Frank admission of costs may help to dampen uninformed support of a program, but it will simplify problems of future accountability.

Full consideration of all aspects of land acquisition is the one way of preventing these problems from ballooning into threats which could alter the fundamental nature of many programs. If those who would reject an open space program because of the emotional problem involved in dispossessing landowners are made fully aware that they will have to face this issue, it is perhaps best to start without them. Their support of the idea may have been of the elementary, emotional type in the first place. Open space parks, like motherhood and environmental quality, have universal support until their costs are explored.

From the time when government development of any type of resource first began, landowners have readily accepted the idea that any added value as a result of the development was their full entitlement. Scandals over the location and purchase price of land for highway construction are the most notorious examples, but locations of all types of public buildings have also traditionally been involved. Reactions of land-owners have varied widely. Some have the notion that they are entitled, as part of compensation, to all the added value which the property would have if they owned it after the government development, even if the government development is the sole reason for the increase in value. Another common gambit is the offer to donate land to influence the location of a project, on the theory that added value to other retained land will more than offset the loss through the donation. The federal government generally rejects such proposals, although this policy is still followed by many local subdivisions. When land costs are an important factor in locating a project, however, bids which have the effect of being donations sometimes become the decisive influence in a decision.

The idea of government directly recapturing some of the value added to property by virtue of a government project is relatively new, although unplanned recapture has occurred at times through sale of land which had become surplus to the project (due to relocations and other changes in policy). TVA first utilized the policy as part of the Beech River project in western Tennessee, where construction began in 1962, and has since adapted it to other programs related to reservoir construction, but including purchase of land for industrial and community development, as planned for the Timberlake community on Tellico Reservoir.

The recapture system has sometimes been attacked as unwarranted government involvement in the real estate business. The attacks on the system have almost always come from those who seek to reap a windfall in added value to their property by virtue of the location of the project.

Though not used by TVA in connection with Land Between the Lakes or other recreation areas, the recapture system has been proposed for park projects. It has value as a means of financing parks or recreation areas which otherwise could not exist. It is no answer, however, to the need for open space free from the distractions of inholdings or the visual pollution which can so often result from the quick commercial exploitation of private land intermingled with park space, or even adjacent to it.

Various other suggestions have been made about methods of easing the difficulty of park land acquisition, but none are likely to be adopted until there is a greater realization of the grave emergency involved in the whole problem. One partial solution would be to allow government purchase, also by eminent domain, of easement rights sufficient to prevent commercial development of properties while government (be it federal, state, or local) is in the process of acquiring land and making it available for public use. Zoning by easement may be a less expensive way of preventing the exploitative inflation of property values, but it needs the experience of practical testing.

The one sure way of acquiring land nearest the minimum of reasonable cost is acquisition well in advance of development, based on detailed planning and projection of future needs. The one way this system can gain sufficient public acceptance is through proper explanation that in the long or the short run it will still save money for the taxpayers. This, of course, will be accepted only when there is universal recognition of the need for planning for open space recreation. The same people who compete for space on crowded beaches or overstuffed campgrounds do not always associate their problem with plans for the next decade. There is no reason, however, why a better explanation of the relationship should not be attempted.

In short, the only solution to the urgent problem of making more open space recreation available to the American people is a comprehensive program by government at all levels to acquire and develop recreation lands and sites. The one way of acquiring sufficient space for these projects will be through the government's power of eminent domain. The purchases are just as much in the public interest as all the previous traditional uses for which eminent domain has been exercised. Costs will be high, but they will be much higher with delays.

The one way to assure a steady progress in meeting open space needs is through the specific allocation of a major sum each year to the purchase of new lands. The money might be used both for direct federal purchase and for division with the states and local subdivisions on a matching basis. But it should be specifically allocated, with a certainty comparable to the funds set aside for the interstate highway program. Trust funds such as these are the one way of assuring a reasonably certain, continuing program.

The money allocated for green space should approximate the amount utilized for the interstate highway program. A ten-year program of one billion dollars a year would not be at all out of line with the priorities involved. It would only begin to meet the long-range need, and the savings in land costs would more than pay for new programs long before the end of the present century.

7

TVA's experience in developing the Land Between the Lakes recreation area in western Kentucky and Tennessee provides no magic answers to the problems of open space, but it does help define the problems and make clear that they tend to accelerate with delay. Land Between the Lakes came into being under the aegis of a government agency with greater acceptance by the local people than any other in the region, but even under these circumstances, it involved more local resistance than any other land-buying program in TVA's history. The story of its development offers lessons for potential developments in other areas, and for the public clientele of such enterprises. The overwhelming acceptance and use of Land Between the Lakes by both citizens of the area and recreationists from many miles around point up the need for similar projects throughout the heavily populated areas of the country.

Chapter Two

Land between the Rivers

THE TWO GREAT LAKES of western Kentucky and Tennessee are man-made, but before them there were the rivers. Nowhere in the United States do two major rivers come so close together without joining. Geologists have no certain answer to the curious physiognomy of the Tennessee and Cumberland rivers, but they agree that some shift in the earth's formations, perhaps during the glacial periods, helped produce the erratic course of these rivers which help the mother Ohio connect Appalachia with mid-America.

The Tennessee and Cumberland rise in the same general area of the Appalachian range, near the eastern boundaries of the states of Kentucky and Tennessee, and flow to the southeast. The direction for both then shifts due west, before abruptly turning north toward the Ohio River just before it, in turn, reaches the Mississippi.

At some point dim in geologic past, while the present Gulf of Mexico was receding to the south, the shifting earth created small ridges now called Hickman and Columbus. These ridges became part of what we call the Highland Rim of the Nashville Basin and helped establish western barriers which moved the two rivers north instead of farther west or southwest.

The Tennessee River turns north after it leaves Alabama and crosses the northeast corner of Mississippi. It does not draw parallel again with the Cumberland until the latter river reaches the point where the town of Dover, Tennessee, is now located. Here began the forty miles of land between the rivers which has now become the Land Between the Lakes.

The land itself was never abundantly rich soil. Although it included a great deal of sandy limestone, a large proportion of chert in the soil limited its productive capacity. Stone which regional geologists refer to as Dover flint is common through the area. This abundant material is of no benefit to agriculture, but made the region attractive to the aboriginal inhabitants of the Mississippi Valley, who would come into the region to make tools and weapons to avoid longer treks east to the mountain rocks. There are traces still to be found in the area of these aboriginal inhabitants who preceded the American Indians. The bivalve mussels they could take from the two rivers were apparently a major attraction.

People of the Mississippi culture are popularly known as Mound Builders, inhabiting both the Ohio and Mississippi valleys for several hundred years until around A.D. 1500. There is some evidence of prehistoric habitation of several periods in the land between the rivers, but the most clearly defined traces have naturally been those of the Mississippi period.

In Stewart County, Tennessee, on the high east bank of the Tennessee, the Mound Builders established ceremonial burial grounds which were evidently used by people from over a wide area. In this vicinity the Mound Builders established a farming community where the inhabitants lived within a fortified village, in some ways similar to the fortified stockade settlements later to be established by European whites as they penetrated into North American Indian country. Corn was the chief crop of these earliest farmers, but artifacts indicate that they fished and hunted more extensively than earlier settlers. Improved hunting and fishing equipment may have influenced the Mound Builders to give up their agricultural life and turn to the migratory search for game.

At any rate, neither the prehistoric nor the Indian population of the land between the rivers was ever large. The area was never identified as containing important settlements of the Shawnee Indians who moved west across Kentucky and the Cumberland Valley, or of the Muskogean tribes like the Chickasaw which became fairly plentiful to the south. When white men came west by way of the Ohio, the Cumberland, and the Tennessee, they established small settlements on the river shores as convenient trading posts with the Indians, but none were located in the territory between the rivers until after the land had become a part of the United States.

French traders were the first Europeans known to have traversed the area, and they entered by boat along the mouths of the rivers. Some followed the Canadian explorers down the Mississippi or west along the Ohio, while others, such as Jean Charleville, who established the first trading post at the site of Nashville, came up from New Orleans.

The Indians had never settled on a name for the Cumberland River that was accepted by more than one tribe. The first French traders called it Louisa, after their king. The explorers from the English colonies called it Shawnee, because that Indian tribe had been located in settlements in the mountains. In 1748, however, Thomas Walker led a party of Virginians in the first formal expedition into what is now eastern Kentucky. Walker renamed the river Cumberland, in honor of the royal Duke, and the name was quickly accepted in the pre-Revolutionary period.

Walker did not enter western Kentucky until thirty-two years later, in 1780, when he arrived as leader of a surveying party commissioned by the state of Virginia to establish the boundary of Virginia and North Carolina west to the Mississippi River. The North Carolina survey party was headed by Colonel Richard Henderson, best known at the time for his land speculations throughout the western portions of both colonial North Carolina and Virginia. On March 31, 1780, the Henderson party, which had preceded overland, was met on the bank of the Cumberland River by a party of settlers from North Carolina, traveling by river to establish a settlement that was to become Nashville, Tennessee. The boatload of settlers was led by Colonel John Donelson. They had come down almost the full length of the Tennessee River, entered the Ohio, and proceeded eastward to the mouth of the Cumberland, which they sailed up and sculled toward Nashville.

The Donelson party took a week to move south against the river current to the vicinity of the North Carolina-Virginia boundary, where they met Colonel Henderson and his men. One of the reasons for the slow progress was the need to kill buffalo and collect herbs along the riverbank to eke out the dwindling rations which they carried.

Even though the two parties met in the midst of their operation, they could not reach agreement on the western boundary between Tennessee and Kentucky. The two states were admitted to the Union with the boundary in dispute, and the federal government left the issue for them to resolve. Numbers of joint commissions were appointed, but for long periods the issue lay dormant while Tennessee refused to recognize the Walker line for the territory west of the Cumberland. The boundary dispute was not settled until 1859. The boundary between the two states moves to its northernmost point in the land between the rivers, some two miles above the boundary to the east. Before crossing the Tennessee River, however, it drops sharply southward.

But neither Donelson, the future father-in-law of Andrew Jackson, nor Henderson was to be more than a peripheral figure in the development of the land between the rivers. The first permanent white settlers came into the area about the same time as Donelson and the surveyors, and several dozen families had established homes and were clearing farms by 1800. Both Kentucky and Tennessee were now states, and settlement in the western portions was being actively encouraged by the state governments.

The land grants between the rivers originated in North Carolina and Virginia, but the cessions of the western lands of these two states to the new national government helped encourage migration to the western end of the rivers. There was little resistance from the Indians, for none had been permanently settled in the region. The one Indian skirmish with whites that took place involved a Creek war party from the Mississippi territory to the south. The Creeks actively resisted American settlement until they were defeated by Andrew Jackson and his troops in the Creek War of 1811-1812, which became part of the War of 1812 for the southern frontier.

Most of the early settlements along the rivers, like the later ones, were on the east bank of the Cumberland and the west bank of the Tennessee. The first of these was Eddyville, where Eddy Creek entered the Cumberland, and near where Colonel John Montgomery, an early associate of Daniel Boone, had been killed by a Creek war party.

Eddyville's best-known citizens were to be among its first settlers. Matthew Lyon came from Ireland by way of Connecticut and Vermont. As a young man he paid his passage to America by becoming an indentured servant, auctioned off for twelve pounds for three years' servitude. He moved north to Vermont in time to work in a foundry for Ethan Allen, and married his employer's niece. He was an officer in Allen's Green Mountain regiment when the Vermont troops made their famous raid to capture Fort Ticonderoga.

In a dispute that developed over army assignments, Lyon resigned from the Continental Army and became the leading founder of the town of Fair Haven, Vermont, where he was the foremost businessman and politician. His political enemies were to charge later that Lyon had been allowed to resign from the army rather than face a charge of cowardice, but his later political career was anything but shrinking from conflict, including physical blows at his opponents on the floor of the House of Representatives.

Lyon was elected to Congress in 1796 and became known as one of the most outspoken critics of President John Adams. In the midst of the American reaction to the excesses which followed the French Revolution, the Federalists passed the now infamous Alien and Sedition Act of 1798. They unwisely chose to make Matthew Lyon their first victim, on a charge of seditious criticism of the president of the United States. Lyon was convicted, but he was reelected to Congress from his jail cell, presaging the overwhelming rejection of Adams and his party at the hands of Thomas Jefferson two years later.

Even though his Vermont neighbors had returned him to Congress, as a Jeffersonian and an outspoken exponent of the soon-to-be-developed Jacksonian democracy, Lyon wanted to live on the frontier. In the fall of 1799 he loaded five wagon teams with relatives, household goods, and supplies from Fair Haven and left for the lower Cumberland, by way of the Ohio River. Lyon bought land and established a trading post at Eddyville and shortly secured through President Jefferson a contract to provide delivery of the mails in the western country. Before long he was elected to the Congress from the western district of Kentucky, and he served three more terms, enlivened by disputes such as one with the Republican leader, John Randolph of Roanoke, of the ethics of Lyon's assuming a government contract to carry the mails in the western country while serving in the Congress. Their debate on the matter is one of the classics of the early Congress, but it had no apparent effect on the status of Lyon's mail contract. It may have influenced his eventual defeat for reelection.

After this defeat, Lyon managed an appointment to a government post in the new territory of Arkansas. He left his son Chittenden behind to look after the family interests in Caldwell County and began a new Lyon business development program in the frontier settlement of Spadra Bluff, Arkansas. He was an unsuccessful candidate for territorial delegate from Arkansas. His political aptitude would have likely made him one of the first members of Congress from this third state if death had not intervened.

Chittenden Lyon had his father's body buried at Eddyville, where the younger Lyon was by far the most prominent citizen. The son eventually was elected to his father's old seat in the Congress, but not before he had built up the family business enterprises and increased the size of the farm until it was one of the largest holdings in the western river country. When a new county was carved from old Cald-well, to include Eddyville as well as the territory west from the Cumber-land to the Tennessee River, it was named Lyon, after Chittenden Lyon.

Although some relatively large land grants and purchases were made during the years before the Civil War, the traditional southern plantation did not become common in the land between the rivers. Most of the farms remained frontier rather than plantation types. Cotton and tobacco were not as much standard farm crops as corn and hogs, and salted pork was a major item for purchase by the river merchants for shipment up the Ohio to Cincinnati and Pittsburgh.

The corn was grown primarily to feed humans, for the hogs could subsist on the nuts and roots of the forest. The wagons and boats which moved west usually carried seed corn and millstones for con-verting corn into meal. Corn was the staple and reliable item of food throughout the frontier period.

Like most of the settlers who came across the Cumberland Gap, or down the western rivers, the pioneers of the area brought hogs with them. As early as 1798 the county court of Christian County, which then included all of the Kentucky section of land between the rivers, ordered that pens be built for the collection of stray hogs. Few farmers penned their pigs, however, but let them feed and root through the open woodland. To protect his hogs, Matthew Lyon, Jr., registered a "stock mark" that consisted of a crop at the top of the right ear and a bit out of the lower portion of the left ear. Hogs were more the common currency of the frontier farmer in this area than the horse, and they were cheap. Papers filed in 1822 in connection with the estate of John Langley of Trigg County valued twenty-six hogs and thirteen pigs at a total of $52. A yoke of steers went as high as $35, while horses ranged from $25 to $110.

Some of the settlers who moved from the plantation country of Virginia and North Carolina brought slaves along, but few were imported for farm work on the land between the rivers. The land and the topography did not lend themselves to large-scale farming and brought returns only through intensive family operations, by contrast with agriculture in other parts of Tennessee and Kentucky. Slaves were a valuable property only if their labor could be used in a productive enterprise larger than the small farmsteads which had been established between the rivers. Even the owners of relatively large holdings often had only a small share in cleared land and farm crops, because the productivity of the land was not rich enough to warrant the investments in large-scale clearing.

THE IRON FURNACE ERA

The development of the iron industry between the rivers brought the first large holdings of slaves into the area. The records are not clear, but the first iron furnace on the lower Cumberland was the one established by Matthew Lyon, who had learned the trade under Ethan Allen. The ore, which the Indians had discovered on the Cumberland rim, had been found by the first white men who came west, and iron furnaces had begun operation in both Kentucky and Tennessee in the 1790s. The Cumberland ore was never of a high quality, but it met the needs for the relatively crude metal products of the frontier. When the ore was found in plentiful quantities between the rivers, iron furnaces were established at a dozen or more spots in the area.

Americans had brought from England the belief that charcoal was the best fuel for the iron furnaces. The abundant forests between the rivers were available to make the charcoal. Fuel and raw material joined to establish the area as the center of iron manufacturing for the South and Middle West.

Most of the major iron furnaces between the rivers were established by men and companies who began their manufacturing activities farther south along the Tennessee River. The most prominent of entrepreneurs were Thomas Tennessee Watson; John and Samuel Stacker, brothers; and Daniel Hillman, Jr. Separately, or in various partnerships, they built half a dozen furnaces and acquired large tracts of woodland to supply charcoal. Daniel Hillman, Sr., had come to Tennessee to work in the iron business, and the Hillman family was to become the biggest name in iron in the South. Daniel Hillman, Jr., named a son Thomas Tennessee Hillman, after his partner, Dr. Watson; and T. T. Hillman became one of the pioneers in the iron industry at Birmingham, Alabama.

The average iron furnace between the rivers was ten or twelve feet wide and about thirty-five feet deep inside. Such a furnace had the capacity to produce from 500 to 600 tons of iron each week, but the average operation was rarely in production more than half a year even during periods of peak demand.

The furnaces used the cold-blast process to separate the iron from the ore, and charcoal was the fuel which supplied the intensive heat necessary. Preparation of charcoal was a tedious process in a day when cutting, hauling, and processing of the wood was done by hand. Carefully cut logs, four feet long, were stacked in cords four feet high and eight feet long. Coal pits would handle about sixty cords of wood at a time. The piled wood was covered with leaves eight inches deep, and this was covered to a greater depth with clay dug from the hillsides. The entire pile of covered logs was centered around a chimney in the center of the pit, which was fired from kindling from the top to start the charring process. A pit would burn for more than two weeks before the charred coal would be ready, always with the danger that some fire-generated explosion in the pit would blow off the leaves and clay and destroy the logs by fire before they were properly charred.

The resulting coal had to be carefully drawn from the pit to keep it from blazing up in the process. It was normally measured by the bushel, twenty pounds to each such container. Two thousand bushels of charcoal were needed to fire the average furnace for a twenty-four-hour period.

The furnaces themselves required relatively small crews for operation, but the need for an assured supply of charcoal brought about the development of a system of each furnace being self-sustaining with a fuel supply crew that included timber cutters as well as charcoal pit operators. The owner, or his designated "ironmaster," usually lived in the vicinity of the furnace, as well as most of the skilled workmen and laborers.

Some of the permanent workmen were recruited from among farmers in the area, and a good part of the wood supply was furnished on a piece-work basis from the same farmers, but the overall operations required importation of labor. The usual procedure became one of contracting for slaves leased from their owners on an annual basis. During the 1840s and 1850s, at the height of iron furnace activity between the rivers, the going rate of pay for slave leases was an average of $150 per year. (Slaves were sold outright for from $600 to $900, so the owners had a good rate of return.) No accurate records exist, but there may have been as many as three thousand slaves working in the iron industry during the 1850s. Some of the iron furnace owners built up fairly large holdings of slaves themselves, but most depended upon leased slave labor.

It was inevitable that the concentration of slaves in the area would produce rumors of slave revolts and insurrection, such as were common throughout the slaveholding South during the last generation of slavery. The worst such panic occurred between the rivers in 1856 and 1857.

In February of 1856 two slaves, a man and wife, were accused of burning a farm storehouse near Cadiz. The husband, listed in the records as George, hanged himself, but his wife, Minerva, was tried and hanged by order of a Cadiz court. The burned storehouse was soon being called evidence of a slave plot, and a vigilante committee was formed to protect against an insurrection. The committee decided that a slave named Solomon Young was plotting a slave uprising and summarily executed him.

Farther south, in Stewart County, Tennessee, the slave plot panic went much further out of control. The existence of a new political party, the Republican, committed against expansion of slavery, may have had something to do with the spread of the rumors, even though there were no Republicans in Stewart County. Three white adherents of the old Free Soil party were remembered, beaten, charged with inciting a riot, and ordered out of the state.

Many slaves did not escape so lightly. Approximately one hundred were arrested in the Dover area, and at least nineteen were hanged, some after trials, and some by summary vigilante action. During the period of panic at least twenty-five iron furnaces were reported to have shut down. United States Senator John Bell of Tennessee, who was to be the Unionist candidate for president four years later, was operating an iron works at the time and was using slaves whom he owned. Nine of them were executed during the insurrection panic, and the senator estimated his loss at $10,000, both from the loss of the slaves and the loss of working time of some fifty other slaves taken into custody at the time.

The last new furnace was built in 1855. New and more efficient methods of processing ore into iron were making the charcoal process less competitive, and higher quality ore was being found and used in other parts of the country. Iron manufacture was to continue between the rivers for some fifty years more, but never after the Civil

War did it dominate the economy of the area, and it was always a declining industry. Continuation of slave labor might have enabled the furnaces between the rivers to have remained competitive for a longer period, but their processes had been outmoded partly because of an improved process first developed near Eddyville.

William Kelly was a dry goods salesman from Pittsburgh, who came to Kentucky by way of marriage to Mildred Gracey of Eddyville, daughter of J. N. Gracey, one of the town's successful tobacco merchants and a diversified investor in other local businesses. With the help of his father-in-law, Kelly began operation of an iron furnace a few miles from Eddyville. The inefficiency of the operation disturbed Kelly, and he soon hit upon the device of introducing oxygen into the furnace by pumping in air, which resulted in more rapid heat reaction as the blast of oxygen met the carbon of the charcoal process. It was a relatively simple expansion of the idea of the blacksmith's bellows, but it worked to increase the production of the furnace and the quality of the resulting iron. Kelly applied for a patent on his process and experimented with it on furnaces on both sides of the Cumberland.

Kelly's father-in-law, Gracey, had little faith in his new process and was reluctant to invest in its improvement or exploitation. Kelly spread word of his process around the country, however, and when the famous English ironmaster, Henry Bessemer, attempted to patent the so-called Bessemer process, Kelly filed a claim of prior invention (in 1847) and clearly hinted that the Englishman had borrowed his ideas. The United States patent office upheld Kelly, and United States Patent No. 17628 was issued to him for the Kelly process on April 13, 1857.

Unfortunately for Eddyville and the region between the rivers, the lack of help from his father-in-law sent William Kelly back to Pittsburgh for help from his father, John Kelly. The son transferred his rights in the patent to his father to forestall creditors in Kentucky. He lost his iron holdings in Kentucky in 1859 and continued his experiments in Pennsylvania. Returns on his patent did not ease his personal financial problems until the 1870s. Eventually, however, the Kelly process and the Bessemer converter united to become a boon to the development of steel manufacturing in the Pittsburgh area, and the former dry goods salesman collected more than $450,000 in patent royalties from steel manufacturers.

Riverboats brought the first settlers to the land between the rivers, and river transportation was an important factor in the iron industry of the region. Riverboat landings became townsites, but most of the landings which became real towns were on the east side of the Cumberland and the west bank of the Tennessee. The ferry was an essential part of transportation for the residents between the rivers, and ferry landing points are still a distinctive part of the folklore of the region. Because of their importance, ferries had to be authorized by the county courts, which usually set their rates. Ferry service was essential, but the amount of traffic was largely dependent upon the routing of the various local roads built by the counties. Despite ambitious plans, roads remained largely local in nature, and the traveler who wanted to make the best time sought the steamboats if they offered a route to his destination.

The same county courts which granted franchises and set rates for ferries also established rates for taverns. Soon after the new Kentucky county of Trigg was created in 1820, the court established the following schedule of rates for taverns:

French or Cognac Brandy	37½ cents per half pint
Rum or Domestic Gin	25 " " " "
Holland Gin	37½ " " " "
Madeira Wine	50 " " " "
Port, Sherry & other wines	37½ " " " "
Peach & Apple Brandies	18¾ " " " "
Whiskey	12½ " " " "
Porter per quart or bottle	25 "
Cyder per quart	12½ "
Lodging per night	12½ "
Breakfast, Dinner & Supper	25 "
Horse for stablage & feeding corn and oats & hay or fodder for	50 "
Same for each 12 hours	37½ "
Same for single feed	12½ "
Oats and corn per gallon	12½ "

Politically, the land between the rivers had little difficulty in the transition from the frontier Republicanism of Matthew Lyon to the frontier Democracy of Andrew Jackson. The Democratic candidates for president traditionally carried the area by large margins, and most of the local politicians of the region were identified as Democrats.

The opposition Whigs were usually dominated by large farmers and planters, and there were few of these between the rivers. In the years just before the Civil War, however, as the Democratic party became more closely identified with the cotton farther south, and its defense of slavery began to include overtones of anti-unionism, the margin of the Democrats in the region began to slip. There was no particular opposition to slavery in the area, but more concern about maintaining the Union than in some other parts of Kentucky and Tennessee. Stewart County, Tennessee, for instance, gave ex-President Millard Fillmore, running as the American, or Know-Nothing, candidate in 1856, 600 votes to the 985 for James Buchanan, the successful Democrat.

When the sectional crisis approached in 1860, the land between the rivers became more conservative on the great divisive issue. The returns from Trigg County west of the Cumberland illustrate the differences of opinion between the rivers and east of the Cumberland. Although John C. Breckinridge, the candidate of the southern Democrats, was a Kentuckian, he received only 184 votes to 221 for John Bell, the Tennessean who was a candidate of the Whig Unionists. Stephen A. Douglas, the Democratic Union candidate, got 128 votes, while the national winner, Abraham Lincoln, got no votes at all.

For Trigg County as a whole, however, Breckinridge scored a small plurality over Bell, 675 to 600. Douglas gained a few votes in the eastern part of the county and totaled 175, while Lincoln received only one vote east of the river.

Chapter Three

War between the Rivers

TRIGG COUNTY'S elected representatives favored secession and attended Kentucky's pro-secession convention at nearby Russellville in November 1861. The Russellville convention, presided over by former Congressman Henry C. Burnett of Trigg County, was called after Kentucky had failed to secede through the action of the regular state government. Two Eddyville delegates from the recently created county of Lyon also favored secession and helped set up the rump state government which supported the Confederacy.

Farther south in Tennessee there is no clear-cut evidence to show a difference in secession sentiment for those who lived between the rivers and those east of the Cumberland, but there is authentic legend of strong pro-Union families who never supported the Confederacy. Federal troops were to win victories in the area in some of the earliest action of the war, but the backlands were to be the scene of irregular action for nearly four years.

Even before Tennessee seceded from the Union, a Confederate officer, Major William F. Foster, visited the Dover area to select a site for a fort on the Cumberland. Fort Donelson on the Cumberland was soon established at the point Foster selected. The first idea for a fort on the Tennessee River was one of the high bluffs on the west side of the river, but artillery officers pointed out that available guns could not be depressed low enough on the bluff to cover the entire river with their field of fire. The otherwise less desirable Fort Henry site on the east side of the Tennessee, just below the state line, was then chosen.

Neither Fort Donelson nor Fort Henry was the most desirable choice for forts to protect the Cumberland and Tennessee rivers for the Confederacy. Their location was largely dictated by Confederate political policy, which deemed it improper to build military installations in a state not necessarily a fully fledged member of the Confederacy. Tennessee, now fully seceded despite a rump Unionist government established in the eastern part of the state, demanded military protection at her northern boundaries. The Confederacy recognized the Russellville secessionist convention concerning Kentucky and seated Burnett as one of its congressmen at Richmond, but it was more willing to defend Tennessee than Kentucky. The result was Forts Henry and Donelson, and this made it necessary for the Union commanders in St. Louis and Washington to look toward the land between the rivers.

President Lincoln wanted to bolster the Union sympathizers in east Tennessee and talked about giving them protection from the west. The eventual result was an order from General Henry H. Halleck, the Union commander at St. Louis, to General Ulysses S. Grant, commanding at Cairo, to mount a demonstration south from Paducah to the vicinity of Mayfield, Kentucky. Grant was told to avoid a general engagement at all costs, and not even to let his own staff officers know that the real purpose of the expedition was to keep the Rebels from reinforcing Bowling Green. The east Tennessee expedition would be delayed for years, but the Grant demonstration took place as planned, without noticeable result.

The stubborn Grant had become convinced of the value of a movement down the rivers, however, and he made a visit to St. Louis to try to persuade Halleck of the merit of such a move. Although he did not admit it to Grant, Halleck and some of his staff officers had been thinking along the same lines from the time he began to receive promptings from Lincoln. On January 30, 1862, Halleck ordered Grant to move on Fort Henry.

Grant was a new type of general to the Union Army in the West. He acted instead of procrastinated. Working closely with Commodore Andrew Foote, he had twenty-three regiments in boats, moving up the Ohio and Tennessee by the morning of February 2. Within a week after receiving the order, Fort Henry would be surrendered. The Tennessee River was above flood stage, and the soldiers on the boats spent the day of February 3 watching farmers gathering their stock along the patches of high ground visible from the river. Groups of Negroes gathered about fires where they had collected the farm stock would shout and wave with pleasure when they recognized the Union troops. Occasionally white refugees came down to the water's edge and asked to be taken aboard the Union boats, where they told of being harassed by Confederate outriders.

Late in the afternoon the troop transports landed on the eastern bank four miles above Fort Henry, where they established an overnight "Camp Halleck." Grant and Foote took four gunboats up the river to within sight of Fort Henry, where they found the flood was all in their favor. Water had covered a good part of the grounds and some of the buildings of Fort Henry, and the rising floods had broken a string of makeshift torpedoes put across the river to stop boats coming from the north. A quick look confirmed reports that Fort Heiman, which the Confederates had begun to construct across the river when it became obvious that Fort Henry was inadequate, was not nearly finished and housed no guns or troops.

Fort Henry looked vulnerable from Grant's command gunboat, but he nevertheless organized an attack which left no room for disruption by unplanned mishaps. Although the gunboats and the forts exchanged occasional fire for three days, the actual assault was held up until February 6, when General Charles F. Smith's division could arrive from Paducah to take over Fort Heiman and be ready to fire into Fort Henry from the gun positions he would assume on the bluff. The actual assault forces would be General John A. McClernand's division. Altogether Grant had 15,000 troops on hand.

The divisions had heretofore existed largely on paper. They were regiments recruited separately, now assigned into line command for the first time, just as they approached their first combat. Most of them were from Illinois, pleased to be commanded by Grant, the West Pointer who had resigned his regular army commission and returned to serve by way of a commission to command Illinois militia.

It rained through the night of February 5, and McClernand's men were quite ready to move after a night without tents. Some of the trails south were flooded, and others were thick with the cherty mud which transformed boots into heavy anchors. The army was supposed to be in position surrounding the fort when the naval gunboats opened up a concerted barrage at noon. The mud, combined with the inexperience of the company officers, delayed the movement long past this hour and left the way open for more than two thousand Confederate soldiers to move out of Fort Henry and east toward Fort Donelson without resistance.

The Confederate brigadier commander at Fort Henry, Lloyd Tilghman, was a capable officer who realized the hopelessness of his position when he first learned of the approaching Union attack. Because of its location on the flooded lands, overlooked by the bluffs across the river, Henry was as much a trap as a fortress. Tilghman later wrote that the site and planning of Fort Henry were so atrocious that "the history of military engineering affords no parallel to this case." His garrison consisted of less than three thousand troops, like their opponents from Illinois facing their first combat. Tilghman held a council of war with his officers on the night of the fifth and ordered most of his command to begin moving out to Fort Donelson and the "real fight" still ahead.

Tilghman himself had been instructed to defend the fort, and his guns and garrison gave a good account of themselves the next day. The Confederate gunners hit Union gunboats fifty-nine times. Only the gunboat *Essex* sustained serious damage, but this prize of Commodore Foote's fleet was effectively taken out of action. The quartermaster and pilot were killed at their posts at the wheel in the pilothouse, and the boat drifted out of action downstream, where it might have been shot out of the water if the Confederates had not had more important targets at the moment.

When it became clear that the bulk of his troops were successfully eluding McClernand's men (even though they had to abandon six field pieces stuck in the mud), Tilghman struck the Confederate colors, to cheers from the Union gunboats. A keelboat from the flagship *Cincinnati* brought the Confederate commander to the gunboat for formal surrender. The water from the river was so high that the sailors rowed their boat through an opened gate of the fort.

Compared with the manpower and casualties involved in later battles such as Shiloh and Vicksburg, which Grant would later fight with the help of the Union gunboats, Fort Henry was a minor skirmish. It was vastly important at the time, however, as a clear-cut Federal victory which knocked out the only Confederate barrier on a river which offered a path south into Mississippi and Alabama, and then east to the mountain ranges which stretched into all the eastern Confederate states. Beyond that, the quick victory left no other course than an immediate attack on Fort Donelson, the Confederate protection for Nashville and all central Tennessee.

Grant's hope that Donelson might become as easy a prize as Fort

Henry soon faded. Even the task of collecting the Confederate supplies abandoned at Fort Henry took several days. To make sure that the Confederates did not return there once his main forces had departed, a garrison was installed under General Lew Wallace of Indiana, and plans were made to improve the fortifications once the flood waters had fallen. General Halleck suggested that soldiers might be spared from this labor by impressing or hiring slaves from the nearby plantations. Grant had to reply that the land between the rivers was different from most of the rest of west Kentucky and Tennessee—there were no plantations, and virtually no slaves.

Good weather and better roads made easier the march on February 12 from the Tennessee to the Cumberland than was the approach up river on the Tennessee bank six days earlier. Still divided in the commands of Smith and McClernand, Grant marched his little army east over two roads—Telegraph road to the north and the Dover road on the south. They reached wooded timberland just out of sight of Fort Donelson in the early twilight and began deployment in a large semi-circle from the west riverbank north of the fort to the river again on the south. A fresh brigade supposed to arrive by boat was not on hand, so Lew Wallace was ordered to leave Fort Henry and come east.

Grant had planned to make his attack on the morning of February 13, with much the same plan he had used at Fort Henry. Foote's gunboats had not all arrived, however, and the assault had to be delayed until they could provide a bombardment of the fort. The day gave the weather a chance to strike a blow. February 12, still unnoticed as Lincoln's birthday, had been sunny and almost warm, typical of the occasional winter hiatus that comes even to the upper South. The army of men marching from river to river was warm and sweaty under the midday sun. Many of the foot soldiers discarded overcoats and blankets along the roadside, where there were no supply wagons to take them to the rear. Company officers and non-coms were still too inexperienced to check such lack of caution.

Twilight came early on the thirteenth, as dark clouds blew over, pushed by a strong north wind. Cold rain fell, soon turning to sleet and snow. The Union army was bivouacked within range of the Confederate guns, so fires were forbidden for either warmth or cooking or boiling coffee. Years later veterans of the campaign still told of standing all night because it was too cold to lie down without cover, describing it as their most grueling experience of the war in the midst of "one of the most persecuting snow storms ever known in this country."

Fort Donelson, better protected than Fort Henry, was a more comfortable encampment for the 18,000 Confederate soldiers inside. The fortifications were much stronger, and the lay of the land made the high water on the Cumberland provide an assist to the defense by blocking off assault from the north because of flooded lowlands and ravines. There were a dozen guns, although only two were powerful enough to do any severe damage to the average gunboat. The fort itself was relatively small, but it was surrounded by an entrenched skirmish line which at the ridge of hills that circled the fort reached south of the town of Dover to protect the more flooded lowlands.

When the first accurate estimate of the size of Grant's attacking force between the rivers, with its supporting gunboats, reached Albert Sidney Johnston at Bowling Green, he immediately sent reinforcements to Fort Donelson, until the defenders outnumbered the Union troops in the first stages of the attack. P. G. T. Beauregard, the other ranking Confederate general in the West, was later to say that Johnston's whole command should have been concentrated around Donelson, to strike and destroy Grant's army before it could move south with any force. Ideally this would have been the best Confederate defense, but Johnston had supply and transport problems which he believed made this impossible. His great gamble to save the middle South from invasion by Union forces would be made two months later at Shiloh, with Johnston himself as one of the sacrifices. The Confederates prepared a vigorous defense of Donelson, but with the knowledge on the part of the high command that they had to prepare for a more massive effort farther south.

Aside from the drive and astuteness of Grant, the vigor of his midwestern volunteers, the greatest handicap for the Confederates at Donelson was the three generals in the line of command at the fort. The command handicap was one of the flaws inherited by the newly organized Confederate army. John B. Floyd of Virginia, who had been secretary of war under President Buchanan, was the ranking general, and he was a general only because he had been secretary of war, and before that, governor of Virginia. Next in line was Gideon Pillow, an elderly veteran of the regular United States Army, who had chosen to take a commission from his native state of Tennessee. Union army officers who had served with him in the Mexican War were pleased that Pillow was not on their side. Third in line was Simon Bolivar Buckner, a native of Kentucky, another former regular officer who had been a contemporary of Grant in the old army.

The gunboats went into action on February 14, but Foote's success at Henry may have helped weaken his tactics in this new assault on a riverbank fortress. He brought his boats too soon within range of the Confederate guns, which returned his fire round for round, and could not be knocked out except by direct hits. Fort Donelson was on higher ground than Fort Henry, and the shore batteries had better fields of fire into the river, with sites prepared in advance for shooting at gunboats. Conversely the greater height of the Confederate position made it a more difficult target for the Union gunboats, whose weapons fired only on a flat trajectory. All four of the gunboats sustained damage, and three of them were virtually knocked out of action. Commodore Foote was wounded, and three of his four pilots killed or wounded. By midafternoon all four of the boats had to retreat northward down the river to avoid being sunk and sustaining more casualties.

The beginning of the ground assault had been planned for the time when the Confederate batteries were silenced. The two armies faced each other all around the perimeter, but only light skirmishing developed on the fourteenth during this artillery duel.

The next day the Confederates took the initiative. The gunboats, at least for the time being, could no longer block their retreat from Dover along the road to Clarksville and Nashville. The only way to save their army was to break out through the Union lines, and that attempt was planned on the morning of the fifteenth. Buckner would initiate a holding action to the north and west, while Pillow, with about 10,000 men, would strike southward at the area held by McClernand's division, force the Union line back to the west, and then hold open a path along the Clarksville road for the evacuation of most of the Rebel forces.

Although the opposing forces were just a few hundred yards apart, scrub timber growth kept them generally out of sight of each other. Most of McClernand's men appeared to be lining up for breakfast in the first dawn when the Confederate assault first struck them. Within a couple of hours blue-clad bodies obscured the snow, and 1,500 men had been killed or wounded in the assault. Pillow's attack had left a gaping hole in the Union line on the south—there were now actually three roads that could be used in reaching the highway to Clarksville.

At this moment, after sweeping the field to the south, Pillow chose to pull back his troops. His later justification for the command was that the men were too exhausted to move forward any further. The Confederates had marched out with full haversacks, with no need to turn back, but at the decisive moment Pillow's characteristic caution and indecision lost most of the value of the attack. Victory was to be transformed into unconditional surrender.

Grant, assuming that it would be his orders that would start the battle, had gone at dawn to confer with the wounded Foote on his flagship, the *St. Louis*. He returned to the shore just at the time the Confederate attack was halted. He immediately ordered a counterattack. McClernand and Lew Wallace had little trouble retaking most of the positions, for most of the Confederates had pulled back in response to Pillow's order.

General C. F. Smith, the aging former commandant of cadets at West Point, had the hardest job in the Union counterattack. His division had to charge the trenches held by Buckner's men. In the saddle, sword upraised, Smith taunted his men to follow him, and they did, straight up the wooded slope that led to the Confederate trenches. When night fell, thanks to Pillow's indecision and Grant's decisive reaction, the trap had closed more tightly around the Confederates.

As Grant rode back to his headquarters, he had to be careful to guide his horse around wounded from both armies still awaiting attention. At one point he saw a wounded Union lieutenant trying to give a drink from his canteen to a wounded Confederate private who lay beside him. Grant dismounted, took a flask from one of his staff officers, and stooped down to give each of the wounded men a deep draught of brandy. He ordered stretchers to be brought up for them. After the general had remounted, he turned and noted that the stretcher bearers were apparently about to take the Union officer and leave the Confederate. "Take this Confederate, too" he told them. "Take them both together, the war is over between them."

Decisions made that night by the three ranking Confederate generals, Floyd, Pillow, and Buckner, were to bring the war to an end for the majority of the Confederate soldiers still in Fort Donelson. Most of them would be destined to spend the rest of the war in Union prisons.

Floyd and Pillow telegraphed A. S. Johnston that they had won a great victory on the fifteenth, which they had, but they were quick to give it up that night in the face of the Union counterattack, and the threat of a new one the next morning. A cavalry colonel from Memphis reported that the Union forces were still a mile from the Cumberland south of Dover, that the flickering campfires in the area were not Federal outposts but the makeshift attempt of both Union and Confederate wounded, stranded by dark, to save themselves from freezing. Professional soldiers like Pillow, however, were not inclined to give much weight to the reports of officers like Nathan B. Forrest, who only a few months earlier had been a civilian with no previous military experience. Floyd felt that the trap had been sprung at Fort Donelson and that only a select few who might board some Confederate transports still held at Dover had a chance to get away.

While secretary of war, Floyd had been criticized for transferring arms and war supplies to army installations in southern states. When these arms were confiscated by secessionist state governments, the criticism mounted to cries of treason in northern newspapers. Floyd feared being put to trial on these charges if he became the first Confederate general captured in the war.

A Confederate troop transport, the *General Anderson,* brought in four hundred reinforcements from Nashville early on the morning of February 16. As his last act as commander, Floyd took possession of the boat, loaded a Virginia regiment on it, and boarded with them after turning his command over to Pillow. Many stragglers were left standing at the water's edge when Floyd refused to let others board.

Pillow was no more anxious to be the first general to surrender than was Floyd. He turned his command over to Buckner and managed to get himself and his staff ferried across to the east bank of the Cumberland on a small flatboat. They rode down the river until they were opposite Clarksville, where Floyd arranged for the *General Anderson* to pick them up. The two generals arrived at Nashville early on the morning of the seventeenth. Pillow later said after the war that he did not believe surrender was necessary at the time Floyd made the decision for the Fort Donelson command, but that the officer who succeeded to command was duty bound to carry out the surrender.

Colonel Nathan Bedford Forrest did not like the idea of surrender either; his plan was for all the troops to march out in the darkness, fighting a path through if necessary. He proved his point by taking his cavalry regiment out through the gap along the river, without casualties. It was the beginning of three years of hairbreadth escapes from the

Yankees, while he rose to the rank of lieutenant general and recognition as the most effective Confederate commander in the middle South.

Buckner had been given the command to surrender and moved to do so before there were further casualties. At three o'clock in the morning he sent an officer into the Union lines under a flag of truce with a request for an armistice and the negotiation of terms of surrender. Grant answered with a brief note that was to become one of the most famous military communications in American history, for it contained the line: "No terms except unconditional and immediate surrender can be accepted."

News of the capture of 14,000 Confederate troops through uncon-ditioinal surrender, removing the only Confederate barriers on both the Tennessee and the Cumberland brought celebrations throughout the North, but particularly in Illinois, from which most of the Union soldiers had come, as well as their commander. In little more than a year's time Sam Grant had been transformed from the failed ex-officer, clerking in a store in Balena, to the Union's first general to produce a major victory. Governor Richard Yates of Illinois came to Dover to join in the celebration. The land between the rivers was temporarily populated by Grant's 28,000 men, 14,000 prisoners, and thousands of newspapermen, "official" visitors, and mere hangers-on—more people than were ever to be present in the area again at one time even after the changes of more than a century later.

The victories between the rivers made Grant the Union commander for the drive to capture the Mississippi Valley, to be climaxed a year and a half later with another surrender at Vicksburg. Fort Henry and Fort Donelson, on the northern border of Tennessee, were the prelude to the terrible, death-laden battle of Shiloh fought two months later on the Tennessee River just above the southern boundary of Tennessee. For the land between the rivers, however, major action of the Civil War had now passed by, even though the rivers themselves would be arteries for troop transports, supply boats, and gunboats for nearly three years yet to come, as Confederate strength remained in middle Tennessee and northern Alabama.

Union forces had to garrison Fort Donelson for the remainder of the war, primarily to make sure that it did not fall into the hands of Confederate raiders. On February 3, 1863, almost a year after its capture, a Confederate cavalry raiding force, headed by General Joe Wheeler with Bedford Forrest as his second-in-command, attempted to retake Fort Donelson. The garrison was alerted before the attack began. Losing the effect of surprise, Wheeler attempted to bluff his way in, with a demand for unconditional surrender. Colonel A. C. Harding, in command of the Union troops, refused to be flustered, however, and replied, "I refuse to surrender the forces under my command or the post without a chance to defend them."

Wheeler gave him his chance, and Harding responded nobly. Although some of the Confederates, dismounted and fighting as infantry, got into the town of Dover, none of them penetrated Donelson itself. Forrest lost two horses, but overall the casualties were light when the attackers withdrew at nightfall. There were no more raids on Fort Donelson.

One of the unpleasant duties of the Fort Donelson garrison was to patrol between the rivers to curtail the activities of the bushwhackers and outlaws who often descended on isolated farms to steal food and other valuables, operating under the guise of Confederate guerrillas or partisans. Guerrillas and unofficial partisan soldiers did operate in much of this section of Kentucky and Tennessee throughout the remainder of the war. They included deserters from both armies, as well as men who had never served in either, using the backlash of the war to cover renegade activities. For some the guerrillas gained romantic fancy, while for others they were merely thieves and robbers.

One well-known but elusive guerrilla who operated on both the Cumberland and Tennessee was Jack Hinson, who owned a large farm on Lick Creek. After his two sons were summarily executed by Federal troops on a charge of bushwhacking near Model, the elder Hinson is supposed to have sworn revenge on every Federal soldier he could ambush. He claimed to have killed thirty-six men, most of them by firing from the shore at Union gunboats and transports moving along the rivers.

Howell Edmonds, perhaps the next best-known guerrilla between the rivers, apparently used this cover to carry on blood feuds with families in the area. He was captured by a Forrest cavalry patrol in 1864 and executed by them a few weeks later.

One of the Confederate raids into the area was led by General Hylan B. Lyon, a member of Matthew Lyon's family. His old neighbors were upset when he came into Eddyville and burned the court house. General Lyon returned to the area between the rivers as part of the command of Bedford Forrest in an extensive raid that reached the site of the abandoned Fort Heiman, on October 28, 1864. The Confederates refortified the heights above the Tennessee with artillery and formidable cavalry support. Another battery was put in position upstream from Paris Landing. The next day the Confederates demonstrated that they had established an effective blockade of the river. Forrest organized a little Confederate navy with captured Union boats and denied effective use of the river to Federal shipping for several weeks. Unfortunately for the Confederates, however, by this time the Tennessee River was no longer an essential supply route for the Union army, and Forrest's horse soldiers could be better used farther south. The great Confederate raider gave up his navy and pulled out of the area for the last time on December 27. During the two months of Confederate occupation of the west bank of the Tennessee, there were no raids across the river or attacks on Union forces on the Cumberland.

Open water surrounds Land Between the Lakes.

Scores of bays and coves mark the shoreline of Kentucky Lake and Lake Barkley.

One favorite activity

Fall color on Kentucky Lake

Campers—

and their activities

Family campgrounds,
lake access areas,
and group camps
provide
a year-round facility.

Shower and rest room facilities at the campgrounds

Architects' models of an outdoor education facility planned for the Conservation Education Center near the Lake Barkley shoreline

An observation tower atop an abandoned silo in the Conservation Education Center

A wooded trail and boardwalk encircle the two and one-half mile shoreline of Hematite Lake.

Among the game animals are *deer, wild turkey, quail, rabbit, squirrel, waterfowl, and raccoon.*

Wildlife photographers, hikers, and birdwatchers frequent the backwoods walks and old logging trails.

An orientation building houses farm implements and tools.

At Empire Farm city children become acquainted with farm animals.

Youth Station—an experiment in outdoor education

At the Youth Station, grade school groups come to live in a natural outdoor setting; during the summer groups of teachers come for workshops.

The crumbling remains of Center Furnace recall another era.

Kentucky Dam

*Kentucky Lake and Lake Barkley form the western and eastern boundary of
Land Between the Lakes. Near the two dams, which lie only three miles
apart, is an open canal that connects the lakes and defines the northern limits of
the area.*

Chipmunk

Beaver

Hiking along wooded trails of the 40-mile-long peninsula

The pileated woodpecker

The cave salamander

Northern cricket frog

Leopard frog

The screech owl and red-tailed
hawk are two common birds of
prey.

A native flock of wild turkey

*Canada goose
and wood duck*

The white-tailed deer, one of the most graceful of all wild creatures, roams freely throughout the area and is often seen along wooded drives and trails.

A small herd of buffalo. American bison once roamed the valleys of the Cumberland and Tennessee in great herds.

The raccoon

The rare white fallow deer

The barred owl

Thousands of Canada geese winter along the Kentucky Lake and Lake Barkley shorelines.

Kentucky warbler

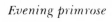

Evening primrose   *Partridge pea*

A fallow buck

Purple fringeless orchid

Butterfly weed

Wild hydrangea

Bluebell

Paper mulberry

Star-of-Bethlehem

Wild hydrangea

Bluebell

Paper mulberry

Star-of-Bethlehem

Shooting star

Wild bergamot

Apricot vine

Blazing star

More than 300 miles of backcountry drives wind through the hardwood forest and along the lakeshore.

Skullcap

Blackberry lily

Recurved trillium

Goat's rue

More than 20 species of ferns have been identified in Land Between the Lakes, including the two pictured here—the blackstem spleenwort and the resurrection fern.

Devil's matchstick lichen

Muskrat

Box turtle

Marbled salamander

A typical embayment and its surrounding fields

Five-lined skink

Green snake

Ribbon snake

Of the almost 3,500 miles of shoreline of Kentucky Lake and Lake Barkley, 300 border Land Between the Lakes.

Fig lichen

Flame lichen

Bristly lemon lichen

Many overlooks provide scenic vistas along the wooded cliffs overlooking Kentucky Lake.

Chapter Four

A Century of Hard Times

During the war there were intermittent efforts to operate some of the iron furnaces between the rivers, but the area had to adjust to a marginal agricultural existence throughout the war. Since cotton had never been an important crop between the rivers, there was little opportunity to profit from sale of this contraband for shipment north, as was the case with former Confederate farmers a little farther south. Many characteristics of the frontier still remained as the nation began to adjust to changes which had come with or been brought to emphasis by the Civil War.

One of the postwar problems was the adjustment to the new role of Negroes as free citizens. The shutdown of the iron furnaces had meant the withdrawal of slave labor from the area at the beginning of the war. One of the difficulties in operating furnaces after the start of the war was slave owners' fears of leaving slaves so close to large blocks of Union troops and the potential for escape to freedom. Most of the slaves were no longer available for lease. When attempts were made to operate some of the furnaces again after the war, the lack of a labor supply proficient at the particular skills of iron manufacture proved a major handicap. The few Negroes who were living between the rivers after the war were farm laborers or farm tenants.

The new conditions under which race was involved in the community became apparent in 1866. Cosby Blane, a Negro who had taken his name from his former master, John Blane, was baptized and admitted into membership in Crockett's Creek Baptist Church in April of that year. Crockett's Creek was the oldest church congregation between the rivers, probably organized before 1820. When the news spread that the church had accepted a Negro member, members of the congregation began to hear adverse comments from neighbors, and before long they began to have second thoughts. In May a motion was made to rescind Blane's admission. In June decision on Blane was deferred, but the church agreed to baptize freedmen in the future "by an order of the church with the understanding that the church will aid the colored race in organizing a church of their own at any time when the circumstances justify."

Then in July a resolution was adopted, again admitting Cosby Blane into the church. The resolution provided, however, that Blane's admission was voted only "with the understanding that we will aid the colored race in organizing them into a church to themselves at this place under the watch care and supervision of the church such to be governed by rules and regulations hereafter to be adopted by themselves." Two years later, in June 1868, the separate church had not been established, and the Crockett's Creek congregation passed another resolution requesting its Negro members to prepare their separate place of worship "as soon as they can." The Negro church was ready for use in the fall, but the white congregation was still bitterly divided over the action which had been taken.

Two prominent members, Orvill Champion and Daniel Vinson, were outspoken in their opposition to the forming of separate congregations. In December of 1868, Vinson was persuaded to withdraw his objections, because "the church was about to break out into an open rupture." Champion would not agree, however, and he finally forced a new church action in November 1869, which formally disposed of his objection in a resolution admitting error in some of the policy which had been adopted, but declaring that it had to be followed "for the peace of the church."

This early attempt at an integration of Negroes into community life thus failed in the first days of freedom. For the future, traditional southern patterns of segregation were generally followed between the rivers.

Churches were the most common neighborhood institution between the rivers throughout its 150 years of settlement. Inexact records make it impossible to estimate the precise number of active congregations at any one time, but there were probably more than fifty for a number of years. Throughout the period, Baptist churches of both the Missionary and Primitive sects were by far the most prevalent, with others present in generally the same ratio as in other parts of rural western Kentucky and Tennessee. Two Roman Catholic churches were established in the late eighteenth century, but no Episcopal church was ever recorded in the area.

The interest in the welfare of the Negroes exhibited by at least part of the congregation at Crockett's Creek gradually disappeared in the face of the economic rivalry in the years after the Civil War. Most of the Negroes were employed by the farmers with the largest acreage, and the affluence of their employers tended to react against them with the remainder of the white community. More and more moved, and those who did not began to be encouraged to do so by vigilante action. The last two Negro families in the Tennessee portion of between the rivers were forced to leave hurriedly in 1905—one legend has it that the last family had to leave bread baking in the stove. Other legends grew that Negroes who happened to be in the area were warned to be out before sundown.

Farther north, in the Kentucky counties, the Negro population also gradually dwindled and disappeared. The one exception was a small community called "Little Chicago," in Lyon County, which was established after Kentucky Dam was built.

The terror of the night rider, in the tradition of the bushwhackers in the Civil War, came back to the region in the wake of the continuing agricultural depression with which the farmers had lived since the financial panic of 1873. As farming increased in importance with the decline of the iron furnaces, tobacco became more and more important as the major cash crop. The small tobacco farmers escaped some of the worst hardships of financing a new system of cotton production, which their neighbors to the south endured, but they failed to benefit from the growing demand for tobacco. Monopoly domination of the tobacco market after the panic of 1873 was one reason.

With rival buyers, agents and factors, the small tobacco factories of the country had to compete actively to supply the expanding market for tobacco that came with population increases and national prosperity. The failure of these companies in the crash, which followed the failure of Jay Cook and Company in 1873, led to the organization of larger companies and an informal monopoly of the marketing system available to tobacco farmers.

The Populist movement of the time was a symptom of the depressed farmers' demand for some type of action to alleviate their hardship. In western Kentucky and Tennessee farmers decided to initiate direct economic action as a more likely method than the political efforts which had failed. The Tobacco Planters' Protective Association was formed in 1905 to regulate the sale of tobacco. At one time the organization claimed more than 25,000 members in Kentucky and Tennessee. Its membership was probably exaggerated throughout its existence, but there was no exaggeration about the violence and fear which came with the Dark Tobacco War which resulted. Robert Penn Warren, a native of the region, has captured the spirit and tragedy of the times in a novel about the war, *Night Rider*.

Despite the large membership in the tobacco growers' association, not all the growers were willing to participate, and many others were not willing to desert the buyers with whom they had traded for years. Sometimes the unwillingness to change buyers was on the basis of mutual friendship, and sometimes the result of financial obligations to the buyer or business interests with which he had connections. Less tobacco was grown between the rivers than in other nearby areas, but because of its very isolation the area was the scene of some of the worst depredations when the tobacco war turned to violence.

The tobacco plant beds of nonmembers on isolated farms were scraped up and destroyed by roving bands of riders. When the county attorney of Lyon County attempted to stop the depredations, a group of masked riders gave him a public flogging, and he fled the state for fear of his life. In 1908 a band of masked men estimated at three hundred collected eleven men from their homes throughout Lyon County, including several from the western side of the river, took them into the town of Eddyville, and gave them a public beating.

Golden Pond was the site of the worst outrages between the rivers. In April of 1907 a band of masked riders burned the village's only tobacco warehouse, which worked with an independent dealer at Clarksville. Eight thousand pounds of tobacco were lost in the blaze. The next year a larger group of masked men appeared at Golden Pond on a ride over the area that included stops at a half dozen farms reported as not cooperating with the association. They took vengeance, not on tobacco farmers, however, but on Tom Weaver, the Negro porter at the Golden Pond Hotel. Weaver was dragged down the street, beaten, and shot.

The tobacco war gradually ended with little success for the association, many of whose members disavowed the terroristic activities of the night riders. The conflict apparently did not involve as much violence between the rivers as it did in other nearby areas, but it left a heritage of night-riding vigilantism which began to plague the region for a long time to come.

A massive raid on the town of Birmingham, on the west side of the Tennessee River, was made in 1908 by approximately one hundred riders, many of whom were identified as being from between the rivers. The ride on Birmingham was apparently as much aimed at Negro citizens of the town as at its tobacco merchants. Every Negro home was reported fired into, and several Negroes were wounded and one child killed. When the Marshall County grand jury began an investigation, two hundred riders appeared in the town in an obvious effort to intimidate the grand jury. Despite these tactics, the jury indicted eleven of the alleged riders. One of them was a prominent physician who lived in Lyon County. He was eventually convicted and sentenced to a year in jail. Prosecution and conviction of some of the terror riders, as well as the belated use of the Kentucky National Guard, eventually halted the night riding.

The terror tactics were of no benefit to the tobacco farmers, but they had the desired effect upon Negroes who lived between the rivers or even immediately across both rivers. During World War II, when the town of Birmingham was evacuated before the site was flooded by Kentucky Lake, only two Negro families remained of what had once been a large black community.

The relatively isolated conditions between the rivers preserved a frontier atmosphere well into the twentieth century. There were no public schools until after the Civil War. In the years after the war approximately one hundred schools were established in the area, all of them log structures except for those housed in churches which happened to be better built. Few of the one-room, country schoolhouses were red, because few of them were ever painted. Sometimes the floors were dirt, but schools in the more affluent communities had puncheon floors, made by splitting logs in half and turning up the relatively flat surfaces to make a very uneven floor. Split tree trunks also served as the base for benches for the students, with the sawed planks usually being reserved to provide long writing desks for the row of students.

By the end of the century most of the subscription schools, where the teacher usually secured his own salary and supplies from among the school patrons as part of his annual assignment, had been replaced by school units which were part of the county public school system. The salary of the teachers averaged around $125 per year, but the school term was rarely more than four or five months.

By the time of World War I, school terms had been extended to six and seven months, and the average teacher salary approached $50 per month. No high schools served the Lyon County region. Some of the grades taught continued up through the high school level, but not in separate schools. Parents who wanted to send their children to high school could make use of boarding schools that were usually several days' travel away. The more common custom was to board an ambitious youngster with friends or relatives in the county seat. The beginning of the automobile era after World War I made possible, for the first time, a comparable high school education for children between the rivers.

One reason the schools between the rivers never measured up to the best of others in Kentucky and Tennessee was the failure of any small town to grow up in the area. Twenty-three post offices existed at one time or another in the Stewart County, Tennessee, portion of land between the rivers. Some survived for long periods, but most were discontinued a few years after being established, because towns failed to develop around the churches, schools, iron furnaces, and stores that were the center of the communities which aspired to permanence as post offices.

Dover, the town on whose outskirts Fort Donelson had been erected, was never a full partner in the area. Model, well into the interior, was the largest Tennessee community between the rivers, and the longest surviving. A real estate development was promoted at the site of the pre-Civil War community of Bass, site of the Great Western iron furnace, in connection with the coming of a sawmill and hopes for an expanded timber industry. A model town was planned, and the post office was consequently named Model when it was established on July 12, 1887. Model never did reach town status, however, although it was the only post office in the Tennessee portion of between the rivers when development of Land Between the Lakes began.

Golden Pond was the one post office to survive between the rivers in Kentucky. It was established in 1848 near a small lake known as the Golden Pond. Theories and legends differ as to why the pond was called "Golden." One is that it contained goldfish; another that it had once been salted with gold nuggets in an attempt to develop a Kentucky gold rush; still another that the setting and rising sun cast a golden glow over the pond; and a fourth, and possibly the most defensible, that a family named Golden had once owned the pond or lived in the vicinity. During the American prohibition experiment in the 1920's, Golden Pond acquired some fame throughout the middle west as the center of a thriving illegal distillery industry whose product brought a premium price as far as St. Louis and Chicago.

The most grandiose scheme for economic and community development between the rivers was also the grandest for western Kentucky throughout the long period of economic drought from the Civil War to World War II. The site for this economic bubble, which excited Wall Street even more than it did the people between the rivers, was the town of Grand Rivers, situated on the narrow ridge where the two rivers almost joined, now just above the canal which connects Lake Barkley with Kentucky Lake.

At the beginning of the promotion, however, Grand Rivers was merely Nickell's Station, where the railroad had come in the 1870s as it moved west to Paducah. The proximity of iron ore and the still unrealized potential of the western Kentucky coalfields excited the imagination of many promoters, both locally and throughout the country. When a promotional group sold the plan to Thomas W. Lawson, the Boston financier who had jousted with John D. Rockefeller, J. Pierpont Morgan, and Henry H. Rogers and survived financially to tell the tale, they brought to between the rivers a place as a footnote in American financial history in the era of the "robber barons."

With its field headquarters in the newly named town of Grand Rivers, the Grand Rivers Land Company bought up several of the old iron furnaces and some 5,000 acres of land. The revived pig iron operation was planned as the stimulus for new industrial development throughout the area, which the company would exploit by the sale of lots and the commercial development of the town of Grand Rivers. The company erected a brick-front building for its office, a hotel, post office, and stores, which Lawson named the "Boston Block." The foundation of the Grand Rivers Land Company was to be the profitable operation of the iron furnaces. Coke made from coal from the nearby coalfields instead of charcoal was to be the fuel for the furnaces, and it was entirely satisfactory. Grand Rivers' location on the Tennessee, with the town planned to spread to the Cumberland, was a major factor in promotion of the company. One of Lawson's ideas was to cut a canal to connect the two rivers to exploit further the use of water transportation.

Within the first year of the operation of the new company the quality of the iron ore available became questionable, and it soon became clear that there was not an adequate supply in Kentucky. After two years the furnaces shut down, and the Grand Rivers Land Company was soon bankrupt. Thousands of speculators throughout the country were disillusioned, but the greatest blow came to the nearly 3,000 people who had moved to Grand Rivers in the hope of sharing in the predicted prosperity.

Henry H. Rogers, the partner of Rockefeller in building the Standard Oil empire, described the Grand Rivers enterprise as part of a general attack on Lawson:

In 1890 the entire country rang with the fame of Grand Rivers, and it was Thomas W. Lawson, of Boston, who pulled the bell-rope. . . . The scheme, as may be deduced herefrom, was a most comprehensive one. The development of the "marvellous deposit of coal and iron," which had been discovered upon the property by Mr. Lawson, one day while seated in his revolving chair in his State Street office, furnished the basis for the incorporation of the Furnaces Company. After $2,000,000 had been "expended," the clamor of the stockholders caused the company actually to build several furnaces. They were erected and stood idle, with nothing to feed them. The whole scheme collapsed in 1892. The stockholders lost every dollar of their investment. . . .

In this, his fourth financial venture, Mr. Lawson did but repeat his former experiences—except, in this case, the loss sustained by those who reposed confidence in his promises was heavier than in any of his prior undertakings.

Lawson later wrote a book called *Frenzied Finance,* an exposé to financial promotion schemes of the period based on his own involvement. In it he defended his role in the Grand Rivers promotion:

The Kentucky experience is one of the pleasantest memories of my life. Measured by dollars and cents it was expensive but was well worth it, as the young man remarked who broke his arm by being thrown from his horse into the lap of his future wife. It makes a long story, and I shall only touch on the leading facts concerning it by way of showing the desperate straits my enemies are put to in their efforts to discredit my career.

My present brokers, Messrs. Brown, Riley & Co., one of the oldest and largest Boston and New York Stock Exchange houses, had floated the Grand Rivers enterprise for some of their wealthy clients. It was an iron, coal, and furnace proposition, and before I ever heard of it, it had been bought and paid for, and enormous furnaces were under way. It was a close corporation. After a very large amount of money—in the millions—had gone into the property, I was induced to take the executive management, and also I put in a very large amount of my own money. My work was to be that of business director, for I did not know an iron or a coal mine from an alabaster ledge in the lunar spheres, and not half as much about an iron smelter as I did about converting whiskers into mermaid's tresses. However, one of the greatest iron men in New England, Aretas Blood, president of the Manchester Locomotive Works, and of the Nashua Steel and Iron Company, was at the head of the enterprise, which apparently safeguarded it. Well, it turned out that there was no iron in the mines—at least not enough to pay for extraction, and the investment simply disappeared. I lost a very large amount—at least, a very large amount for me—but I had to show for it the love and friendship and respect of the inhabitants of one of the fairest places on the earth—a place where brave men and lovely women live in peace and comfort in the knowledge of their own fearless, simple honesty, and their hatred of shams and trickery—in absolute ignorance of frenzied financiers and the "System's" votaries.

The history of Grand Rivers is an open book. There is no secret about my connection with the enterprise. It was a straight and proper venture. The men who are my brokers of to-day fathered it, and they are men of honor, probity, and responsibility, who since my first year in business in 1870 have been my close business associates and personal friends.

Occasional iron furnaces operated intermittently between the rivers until World War I, but only for a few years at a time and with limited employment. Many of the large landholdings which the iron furnaces had acquired for charcoal sources became part of even bigger holdings as they were acquired by lumber companies for occasional timber-cutting operations. Others reverted to the states of Tennessee and Kentucky for taxes. The state of Kentucky established one of its first game reservations on one holding it had so acquired.

The coming of the depression of the 1930s brought little change to the area, for the land between the rivers had been in depression, except for the iron furnace operations, from the time of its first settlement. One of the New Deal land reform agencies, the Resettlement Administration, bought several of the large tracts with plans for a farm resettlement program. The land proved of such poor quality for general agriculture, however, that the farm resettlement program was never carried out. The holding, together with the Kentucky game reservation, was made a part of the National Wildlife Refuge System in 1938.

A major change came to the area for the first time in 1945, when the Tennessee Valley Authority completed the building of Kentucky Dam on the Tennessee River just a few miles north of Grand Rivers. The change from a river to a lake sharpened the eastern shoreline of Kentucky Lake and covered most of the site of old Fort Henry, but otherwise had little physical effect on the eastern shore. New industrial development came to the area in places like Calvert City, and a flourishing resort business developed on the western shore of the lake. People between the rivers found employment in the new industries and businesses. Some moved out, and others commuted to work.

Kentucky Lake changed the face of western Kentucky. The stimulus of a changing landscape stirred many of the small towns to seek diversified industrial development. The example of Calvert City made it clear that the region could develop and train the skilled labor needed for both heavy and light industry. Many small businesses were either established or expanded to serve the growing recreational demand. Other industries located in the general area because the attractions of the reservoir would help assure a stable labor supply.

The people who had felt the economic stimulus of Kentucky Lake were chief among the promoters of the idea of a dam on the Cumberland River to work in tandem with Kentucky Dam on the Tennessee. Because the Cumberland was a responsibility of the Corps of Engineers, separate from the TVA territory, the Congress authorized a dam to be built by the Corps thirty miles above the mouth of the river, according to a Corps plan to construct and operate it in close coordination with Kentucky Dam.

Chapter Five

Land Between the Lakes

THE FIRST FUNDS for the construction of Barkley Dam were appropriated by Congress in 1955, but delays in appropriations were to hold up its completion for a full ten years. As the work progressed, however, people began to think about a program to use fully the new project in conjunction with nearby Kentucky Dam and Lake.

There was no great problem of coordination for the operation of the dams and locks. A canal across the narrow neck between the rivers, just south of the town of Grand Rivers, would connect the two lakes, which would be maintained by the Tennessee Valley Authority and the Corps of Engineers at the same pool levels. This would require coordination of the operation, which in turn would improve the capacity of both structures to help provide flood control for both the Ohio and Mississippi valleys.

The proximity of the two locks on the two rivers, with the connecting canal, became a navigation asset for both river systems. River traffic could then benefit by the interchangeability of routes, and the two locks could function as alternates to avoid tie-ups during periods of heavy barge traffic.

The canal between the lakes would not be wide, but it would complete a man-made peninsula extending from west Tennessee north across most of west Kentucky. The land between the rivers would become the land between the lakes, separated from the rest of the countryside by two large reservoirs which man had created from the rivers, and cut off at its northern tip by the connecting canal. The geography of the region had been unique from the beginning, and now man's work was giving it an even more distinctive setting. People between the rivers, in nearby Kentucky and Tennessee, and in some of the responsible government agencies began to think about the future use of this old land holding new opportunities and new possibilities.

One result of concern about the future was the organization of the Twin Lakes Development Association, composed of people from the general vicinity of between the rivers, from both Kentucky and Tennessee. The organization had no specific program and never reached any permanent status, but it indicated the interest of the people in making the best possible use of the land.

A meeting of the organization was held in September 1958, along with representatives from private industrial concerns and government agencies, to discuss potential development in the area and to offer assistance in the planning. The general consensus of the gathering was that coordinated planning between public and private groups was necessary for full realization of the recreational and industrial potential of the area. A specific request was made for planning assistance from the planning agencies of both Kentucky and Tennessee. One of the results of this request was a report prepared by the Tennessee State Planning Commission entitled "Report on the Effects of Barkley Reservoir and Cross Creeks National Wildlife Refuge on Stewart County, Tennessee."

Cross Creeks National Wildlife Refuge was to become the replacement for lands within the Kentucky Woodlands Wildlife Refuge which Barkley Lake would inundate. There was concern in Stewart County, Tennessee, about the extent to which this acquisition would conflict with potential industrial development and possible recreational use and development of the new lakeshore.

In preparing the report for the Twin Lakes Association and for other interested people in Tennessee, the State Planning Commission called in for consultation responsible staff people from several government agencies. The plans did not directly affect the Tennessee Valley Authority, but TVA staff people were consulted because of their long experience in water-based recreational development at nearby locations.

Recreation had been the largely unforeseen bargain in the whole Tennessee Valley development program. The TVA system was authorized by Congress on the basis of potential flood control, navigation, and power benefits, to be enhanced by the coordinated development of these benefits throughout the Tennessee River system. There was no mention of recreation development in the law establishing the Authority, but the recreation benefits began to become apparent soon after the first reservoirs became operational. TVA developed a system of reservoir and shoreline operation to assure a broad use of the recreational potential by the general public, and the staff members assigned to this work soon were recognized as among the most skilled in the nation.

By the end of World War II, fishing, boating and swimming in the TVA lakes had become the most important aspect of the Authority program to many citizens, including thousands of visitors from many other sections of the country. TVA recreation specialists had played an important part in promoting these interests by making the facilities available to the public in the most attractive ways, but they had never had a chance to work on a project where outdoor recreation was the major conservation goal.

The land between the rivers, about to become the peninsula between the lakes, offered unique opportunities for a new type of recreation-based program. The relatively primitive condition of the area, now about to be reinforced by the isolation of water on three sides, made it the best available site in mid-America for recreation development built around conservation concepts. Using U. S. Route 79 in Tennessee as a southern boundary, except for a curve eastward along the ridge beginning at Bear Creek in order to exclude the relatively urban area of the town of Dover, the peninsula included approximately 170,000 acres, of which nearly 70,000 were already owned by various agencies of the federal government.

Harold Van Morgan was one of the TVA officials in the Division of Reservoir Properties who was involved in the discussions with the Tennessee Planning Commission in the preparation of the Stewart County report. After he began to study the area as a result of these discussions, Morgan began to develop a plan for its use that fitted its unique characteristics. Why not use the whole peninsula for recreation development? Morgan discussed his idea with other staff members and presented the idea to the TVA board of directors. Eventually the plan was approved by the board and submitted to President Kennedy for approval as part of his program.

The plan was for a national recreational area, developed and operated with the purpose of emphasizing conservation values and conservation education as an aspect of recreation. The TVA report to the president also stressed the value of the economic stimulus to the area which construction and operation of the facility would bring. Development "will have a sustaining influence on state and privately operated recreation attractions on the west shore of Kentucky Lake and on the east shore of Barkley," the directors pointed out. "It will stimulate tourist and recreation travel to a far greater extent than would any number of private developments within the area. Its development and use for recreation will be conducive to more industrial development at Calvert City, Kentucky, and elsewhere in the vicinity."

The report pointed out that most of the federal recreation lands were in western national forests and parks and that relatively few existed in the central United States. The land between the lakes was within 500 miles, or a day's automobile travel, of more than 70 million people. Use of the land for recreational development was the logical and best use, not only for the people in the general vicinity but for all the people of the United States. The TVA directors pointed out that the area involved "has few natural resources for economic development other than recreation. It has been sparsely developed. Its principal asset is the cove-studded shoreline resulting from the federal investment of nearly $300 million in the Barkley and Kentucky projects."

While the report did not spell out details of a program, it pointed up the relatively sparse population of the area, estimated at less than 5,000 people with about 1,300 dwellings. (The actual totals proved to be about 950 families representing approximately 2,700 people.) The governors of both Kentucky and Tennessee endorsed the proposal. Members of Congress representing the area had also endorsed it and proposed that TVA be given the responsibility for the development.

President Kennedy referred the report for consideration by other federal agencies with related responsibilities. After detailed consideration, they joined in approving the idea. The president formally indicated his approval by submitting a request in June 1963 for a supplemental appropriation of $4 million for the fiscal year beginning July 1 for TVA to begin work on the project. The appropriation was approved by Congress without objection in the regular TVA appropriation bill late that year.

One of the first decisions made by the TVA board of directors about the new project was the actual name for the development. The choice was natural and logical. For the people of Kentucky and Tennessee the site had been known for one hundred and fifty years as "between the rivers," and sometimes "land between the rivers." Now that the rivers were becoming lakes, the only logical name was Land Between the Lakes.

Another essential decision was related to this concept of an isolated area, defined on three sides by water. The TVA directors made an early decision that proper development and operation of Land Between the Lakes would require full ownership of all the land between the lakes, with Highway 79 in Tennessee as the southern boundary, except for the curve north and east around the town of Dover.

Exclusion of private property from Land Between the Lakes was a natural response to the plans to emphasize conservation values in recreation. Private "inholdings," no matter what their original use, would inevitably lead to defacements to the landscape such as those adjacent to many national parks today. Beyond the defacement, there would have been the possibility of questionable entertainment enterprises being operated in the midst of a recreation center designed primarily for family use. The man-made physical water boundaries of Land Between the Lakes offered an ideal chance to establish a natural isolation for the area. Any decision not to use fully the boundaries would have lost one of the major natural advantages of the site.

Many property owners within the area, as well as would-be promoters, were bitterly disappointed by the decision. Dreams of windfall profits from sharply increased land values were shattered. Some of those who had been foremost supporters of recreation development between the rivers now became opponents of Land Between the Lakes, but others saw both the reality and the justice of the decision and accepted it as part of the procedure to enable Land Between the Lakes to reach its fullest potential.

A major influence on the TVA decision was the knowledge that inholdings in national and state parks are a major source of public dissatisfaction in both appearance and operation. George B. Hartzog, Jr., director of the National Park Service, described inholdings as "the worm in the apple" for public parks. Hartzog knows the problems well, for only seven national parks are completely in public ownership. "On private lands within parks you will find lumberyards, pig farms, gravel pits, logging operations, and sheep and cattle ranches," he reports. "Plus power plants and mine shafts, auto junkyards, garbage dumps, private plane landing strips, and proliferating residential subdivisions." Hartzog might also have mentioned short-order drive-ins, nightclubs, saloons and even less reputable establishments, all of which have been reported in the midst of public parks, often on the direct access roads to their main attractions.

Delaying purchase of parts of parklands has proved to be a costly and self-defeating device of approaching the land acquisition problem. A classic example of poor economy involved a tract of 163 acres in Yosemite National Park, California. The land was purchased for $2,550 in 1948 at a county tax sale. The owner turned down a Park Service offer of $15,000 for the land in 1951, but gave an option for purchase at $20,000 in 1956. Interior Department officials in Washington thought the price was too high and refused permission for the Yosemite officials to buy it. The park superintendent asked permission to start condemnation proceedings before the tract was divided up and sold in quarter-acre lots, but this authority was denied.

After the residential development actually got underway, the Park Service offered $175,000 for the land, but the offer was refused. Condemnation proceedings finally started, and the inholding finally came into the park at a purchase price of $265,000, with no estimate available for the endless manhours spent in working on the transaction in the seventeen-year period.

TVA selected one of its senior staff officials, Robert M. Howes, to be in charge of the development of Land Between the Lakes. Initial planning was begun at the Knoxville office, but the entire operation was moved as soon as possible to a headquarters between the lakes. A number of conservation education and recreation specialists from throughout the country were consulted in the initial planning, but a special effort from the start was made to attract qualified people from the Land Between the Lakes area to apply for work with the project at all levels.

From the start all the TVA officials accepted the idea that Land Between the Lakes, to be the viable demonstration of conservation and recreation for which it was conceived, would never be confined to a rigid, fixed pattern of development. To achieve its purpose, it would have to be designed with enough flexibility to meet the changing needs in the field, especially in relation to the role of a federal demonstration designed to help establish precepts for the successful operation of similar facilities by state and local governments, as well as other federal agencies.

Some basic concepts became clear, however, and were adopted as policy for Land Between the Lakes. Modifications of early specific ideas have become an inevitable part of the process of the development of the project, but the basic premise of the early concepts still holds up as operational experience lends maturity to the Land Between the Lakes demonstration.

The United States has always been a land of outdoor recreation. Not only the native Indians, but Americans of every racial extraction and cultural background have hunted and fished for pleasure and adventure as well as for food. Just as people learned to earn a livelihood from the land, they have learned to return to it as a source of rest, relaxation, and pleasure during leisure hours. Fields and forests, streams and lakes, mountains and prairies generally have been open to Americans for all types of outdoor recreation, as part of one of the nation's great traditions. For the first one hundred and fifty years of the nation's existence, more than half of the nation could find recreation close at home in the "lower forty," or the upland pasture, or down the hollow. Even for those who had moved to town, there was open space at the foot of Main Street, or at the end of the carline—or at least in one of the vacant lots that seemed to be on every block. Even the first of the big cities were close to the countryside in the days before the automobile ended the era of sharply defined city boundaries.

Changing conditions and habitat not only have urbanized the vast majority of the population but have denied access to the open country-side for those whom the automobile has given greater mobility than their counterparts had in the past. Public lands and waters have become essential if outdoor recreation is to be available to more and more people. This change has come so rapidly, combined with a vast increase in the percentage of the population with both leisure time and money to invest in recreation, that there has still been no adequate experience in the best means of providing adequate outdoor recreational opportunity for the entire population.

Land Between the Lakes would mean that for the first time under federal administration all the resources of an area of reasonable size would be managed and cultivated to produce the most favorable possible environment for outdoor recreation. (National parks of necessity have been limited largely to viewing, rather than the more active personal pursuits.) As part of the cultivation of the outdoor recreational environment in Land Between the Lakes, roads, trails, beaches, campgrounds, picnic areas, and other facilities would be provided for both a proper setting and support for outdoor recreation with special emphasis upon conservation values. To maintain the magnificent natural setting, techniques of multiple-use land management would be employed to improve the area's forest cover and to provide food and shelter for a more abundant wildlife.

From the start the recreation demonstration was designed to help provide a unique outdoor conservation classroom and laboratory for those who like to mix their outdoor recreation pursuits with an educational flavor. Land Between the Lakes was envisioned as an area to which the public would be invited to come and do, as well as to come and look; where the urban dweller would have an opportunity to renew and maintain his contact with the land, the water, the forest, and wildlife in its natural habitat. Programs would be evolved where student and even adult groups could have the actual experience of planting trees and working on other practical projects designed to heal the scars of erosion and improve the natural beauty of an area. The overall Land Between the Lakes program would also include a more direct type of experience for those interested in the actual process of harvesting timber—the chance to relearn the healthy skill with an ax and hand-tools that were once part of the overall educational process for almost all inhabitants of frontier and rural America.

Beyond the entertainment and education of the thousands of visitors, however, Land Between the Lakes was envisioned as a positive, dynamic factor in the continued economic development of the Tennessee Valley and the nation as a whole. It would show that an area having only limited natural resources for conventional and traditional forms of economic growth and development could achieve special stimulation for economic growth through the development of a public recreation area. Although private business would be barred from the actual operating area of the Land Between the Lakes, the overall operational policy would provide active encouragement to private enterprise for investment in motels, resorts, restaurants, and other commercial facilities on the opposite shores of both lakes and along the various highways approaching the entrances to the facility.

A careful estimate, based on previous experience in related developments, indicated that as much as $25 million would be invested in the vicinity for "bed and board" facilities, with other recreation services and attractions offering additional possibilities. This investment would result in the creation of at least 1,500 new jobs in food and housing enterprises to serve the visitors to Land Between the Lakes.

Perhaps an even more important part of the economic benefit of the project was expected to be more indirect. The increased market for recreation-related items among consumer goods would be reflected in increased activity in already established mercantile and distribution centers in the area. For industrial development not related to recreation, the expanded recreational opportunity would be an invaluable community asset in attracting technical and managerial personnel, as well as all types of skilled labor, and helping to provide a stable labor market. Previous experience has shown these items to be a major factor in long-range planning for some of the nation's most successful and aggressive industrial enterprises.

TVA made clear from the start that the adjacent areas which would profit most from the economic benefits of Land Between the Lakes would be those which most actively planned for fullest use of their human and land resources. The countryside would have to be protected from quick commercialism which would destroy the opportunity for planned industrial plant sites. The overall quality of the environment would have to be maintained and improved if the industries attracting skilled, high-wage workers and technicians were in turn to be attracted. There was no tradition of either planning or zoning in most of the areas adjacent to Land Between the Lakes, but TVA hoped that the local government and local leaders would take the essential steps for long-range planning necessary to achieve the economic potential.

Although the Kentucky Woodlands Wildlife Refuge would be absorbed, TVA regarded Land Between the Lakes as an opportunity to increase the amount of land and water for migratory waterfowl while simultaneously increasing the available food and shelter for deer and many species of small upland game. As an integral part of the project, new habitat areas would be made available for many varieties of wildlife, with especial emphasis on waterfowl, turkey, and deer. Special pond-size impoundments in former creek bottoms would provide additional opportunities for fishing, to contrast with the open lakes.

New forest clearings and special cultivated areas would provide both food and shelter for small upland game. These new features would be located close enough to roads, trails, and campgrounds to make it possible for visitors who were not skilled woodsmen to observe wildlife at all seasons of the year. Nature trails would be built around small ponds (some preserved from old farm ponds), with facilities for late evening and early morning viewing of the wildlife. Fishing, of course, would be available in all seasons, and hunting would be a regular feature under carefully planned, appropriate conditions.

General planning for Land Between the Lakes began immediately after President Kennedy directed TVA to assume responsibility for development, but detailed planning and preliminary construction could not begin until January 1964, after President Lyndon Johnson signed the bill appropriating the first funds for the work. Each modification plan involved a new problem but also a new opportunity for meeting the goal of a demonstration of the value of conservation-oriented recreation to a region and to the nation. TVA expects modifications and adjustments based on experience and changing public needs to continue throughout the development of Land Between the Lakes. Even after development is relatively complete, changing national needs and public demands will probably mean changing emphasis and regular restructuring of the facilities. Land Between the Lakes is expected to be a living demonstration that the federal government, responsive to the needs of the people of the nation, can provide a facility which will be a constant contributor to the improving quality of life for the American people.

Chapter Six

Plans to Reality

THE FLEXIBILITY provided by the original TVA Act gave the Tennessee Valley Authority both the freedom and the responsibility to put into action the plan for Land Between the Lakes. TVA's experience in relocating families and communities before building dams would prove invaluable in the relocation program essential for a man-made and man-restored recreation area. The one inescapable hardship was the fact that family homesteads of many generations would have to give way to a new public purpose. Every effort would have to be made to soften this blow for these people. Schools, businesses, churches, lodges, and various other institutions and organizations would have to be disbanded as their members and patrons left the area. Power and telephone lines, some only recently installed, would no longer be needed. Arrangements would have to be made, and made quickly, to acquire land, help families and businesses to relocate, adjust governmental and utility services, and ease community adjustment problems. Speed was of the essence to lessen the agonies of relocation as well as to clear the land for construction that was to follow.

Other forces also demanded speed of action. Along the eastern boundary to be formed by Lake Barkley, land was still dry. Earth could be moved by bulldozers to create new harbors, build small dams, relocate lakeshore roads, and shape the future shoreline for useful recreation purposes. Once the reservoir was impounded, work could be done only by dredges or draglines at a cost that would probably be prohibitively high. Moreover, the schedule within which work could be accomplished "in the dry" was already established, not by TVA and the Land Between the Lakes program, but by the Corps of Engineers' Barkley Project. The schedule, though later held up because of delayed appropriations, called for impoundment of Lake Barkley by the fall of 1965, a schedule that left only months for preparation.

Still another driving force was the goal established by the TVA board of directors, that the first Land Between the Lakes facilities would be available for public use during the 1964 recreation season. Made in good faith at a time when there was no reason to anticipate undue delay in receiving the necessary appropriations, these assurances were interpreted by the TVA staff to constitute a commitment to be honored if humanly possible. The first component, the Rushing Creek Campground, was opened to the public on June 1, 1964.

TVA had to establish a staff to plan and administer Land Between the Lakes, and the nucleus was available within the existing Division of Reservoir Properties, which has responsibility for recreational development and management throughout the TVA system. The decision was made to create a separate division to administer Land Between the Lakes. Such an organization could use the tested skills and working methods reflected elsewhere in the TVA organization. The division would be accountable to the general manager and board for bringing these skills together in a coordinated attack on the job to be done in Land Between the Lakes. Robert M. Howes, chosen to head the division, was a knowledgeable and enthusiastic outdoor recreationist himself, familiar with related programs throughout the country.

The TVA staff organization constituted a clear and manageable assignment of a defined responsibility undiluted by the distracting and sometimes conflicting responsibilities that inevitably impede the progress of committees trying to do tasks that require the direct hand of a single administrator. It placed the Land Between the Lakes program directly under the general manager, squarely in the line of command, yet close to the TVA board whose members felt a direct and personal concern with the program. In the words of one member, "The Land Between the Lakes assignment is the most exciting on TVA's current docket." Each board member saw in the program a challenge far exceeding the opportunity merely to provide needed camping facilities for the traveling public or more acres of open space to which people might escape. The TVA board saw in the Land Between the Lakes program a means of helping the American people maintain contact with the land (broadly defined to include the total environment).

In January 1964 Land Between the Lakes was established as a demonstration project, with division status in TVA. The Land Between the Lakes organization then needed to be filled with people qualified for its key positions. These people had to be familiar with the TVA organization and its working methods. They had to possess in-depth background in recreation resource development problems. They had to know the Land Between the Lakes area and its setting. As a group they must have had a variety of successful experience in solving the wide range of practical problems that lay before the program. Perhaps most important, they had to be equipped with a philosophical capacity to discern the opportunity for meaningful innovation. Practical demonstration was essential in the field of recreation use of resources, a field more blessed with knowledge of what not to do than with examples and demonstrations of how to do it.

TVA found most of these people within its own organization, most of them within the Division of Reservoir Properties. Collectively, the group initially assigned to the program had accrued more than a century of experience with resource development in the Tennessee Valley, well over half of which was concerned directly with recreation resources. Experience among the group had not been confined to the central offices in Knoxville, but throughout the Valley. It included a broad exposure to the experience of other agencies with whom the group had worked in the local, state, national, and even international levels. Many employees were brought in fresh from college, and plans were set in motion to employ many students while they were still in school. Support positions were staffed only in part from within TVA. Many were recruited from elsewhere in the federal government and from states, universities, and private businesses. A further safeguard against possible inbreeding from too much internal recruiting was the employment of consulting services from recognized authorities throughout the nation.

Within six months, accountability for the Land Between the Lakes program was vested in the hands of a viable organization whose responsibilities had been defined and assigned to newly designated staff. To these people was given the task of simultaneously translating the concept into a workable program, carrying out detailed planning, bringing about acquisition of the necessary properties, assisting in the relocation of displaced families and businesses, securing the design and construction of the required improvements and facilities, and operating these upon completion. Small wonder that those involved and who remained involved still regard the Land Between the Lakes program as the most exciting and challenging job in their field in the entire country.

Knowledge of the Land Between the Lakes program and its implications had become general in western Kentucky and Tennessee by the time it got underway in 1964. Meetings of public officials, such as that held in August 1961 and attended by the secretary of the interior, the governors of Tennessee and Kentucky, and various other officials from the federal and state governments, had been widely reported in the local and metropolitan press. Each important development was reported by the press of the area.

Solid knowledge, however, was obscured by rumors and the sometimes conflicting viewpoints that were expressed from both within and outside the area. For the average person, fact was difficult to isolate from fiction. Possibilities and probabilities became confused with actualities. Most citizens knew as much as they wanted to know: "We hear the federal boys are creating new recreation opportunities in west Kentucky and Tennessee. This is good. We are glad they are doing something about it. Someday we'll go down and enjoy ourselves."

This knowledge, however, did not satisfy those who would be most directly affected—the residents, homeowners, and property holders between the rivers. The questions were obvious, but no less serious because of their obviousness: "If my home and property are required for the new program, when will it be? What and when will I be paid? When and where will I move? Where can I turn for help? If I don't want to sell, will I have to sell? Can the government take my property anyway? If so, under what conditions?" These questions affect individuals and families and can be answered only according to the particular circumstances of that individual or family.

Still other questions were of a community nature: "As my neighbors move away, what happens to the church where I worship? What happens to the cemetery where my people are buried? How will my children get to school? Will there be doctors and hospitals when I need them? Will the roads now maintained by the county remain open for me and my neighbors to travel? Will tourists, vacationers, and fishermen—all strangers—understand and respect the rights of all of us to whom this area is home?"

The quickest and best answers could be provided by the immediate work of detailed planning, construction, and operation, which gave added impetus to the determination to get the program underway. The concept of Land Between the Lakes was certainly not overburdened with details. Its dozen or so pages and two maps were free-ranging in their suggestions for possibilities and offered few words of qualification to limit the imagination. Few government documents, perhaps, have launched more with fewer words.

Acclaimed as an engineering organization versed in the ways of blueprint and drafting tables, TVA was well aware of the indispensability of sound planning and engineering. It was also aware of limitations of detailed specifications. A dam may be blueprinted to handle specific volumes of water and to generate specific amounts of electricity. An airport or a bus terminal or a highway can be designed to channel specific numbers of people, or the vehicles in which they travel, past a given point at a given time. But a program attempting to meet an unfulfilled aspect of the holiday needs of the American people with any such degree of exactness would only find itself straitjacketed.

Instead, TVA has expanded its original concept for Land Between the Lakes not into a master plan but into a planning program that is not yet finished and, hopefully, never will be. Unlike a master plan encrusted with unnecessary details, the planning program remains flexible, responsive to the federal budgeting process, to changing developments in the surrounding region, to increased knowledge about the area, to increased knowledge of conservation ecology, to changing recreation habits and technology, and even to the fads of outdoor recreation.

Federal budgeting is a continuous process that some have compared with the flow of a glacier. Glacial or not, it is designed to reckon with the complexities of government in a rapidly changing world. In a succession of annual, biennial, four-year, and five-year cycles it produces —and requires—a steady stream of words, pictures, maps, and figures to which no master plan could be completely responsive, either internally or externally.

If the Land Between the Lakes program does its job, it will bring about changes in the surrounding region that may well have a rebounding impact upon the program. The concept, for example, visualizes an ultimate demand for 5,000 family camping units to serve the visitors attracted to Land Between the Lakes. But will all of these be required within its boundaries, or will private enterprise find it profitable to build some of them outside the boundaries, on the opposite lakeshores? Some are already being built as private investments. The planning program remains flexible on this point.

A writer in the late 1930s could say about the area now known as Land Between the Lakes only that, "West of the Cumberland River (toll 30 cents) is a sterile region."[1] This is the same area now extolled as a "land of enchantment, a vacation paradise, an accessible wilderness, America's answer to the leisure revolution"—quite a revolution, at least in the evaluation of a piece of real estate.

When the Land Between the Lakes concept was evolved, knowledge about the area had increased substantially beyond that available to the writer in 1939—adequate enough to support the concept and to launch a program—but it was hardly adequate for a master plan to which future development would be committed. Even now, basic information concerning the area's history, its plants and animals, its springs and water courses, its geologic features is still coming in. Certainly not enough is yet known about its ecology on which to commit details of future plans. Only a planning program, not a master plan, can remain responsive to increased knowledge about the area.

America's leisure revolution is still primarily a revolution of change. The findings of the Outdoor Recreation Resources Review Commission, completed as the concept for Land Between the Lakes was being generated, are still valid in general but outdated in detail. Campgrounds designed only to this year's catalogs of camping equipment will almost certainly have to be redesigned to meet the requirement of next year's. Nor is there any doubt as to rising expectations of campground patrons. Each year's innovations can be counted on, not to satisfy expectations, but to generate new ones.

THE DEVELOPING CONCEPT

Land Between the Lakes is not burdened with a master plan. In its place has evolved a planning program that charts directions of efforts but does not inhibit or stultify innovation. The original concept called for campsites to accommodate 5,000 parties. It was thought that these would be grouped in campgrounds of 300 units or more. A few

[1] W.P.A. *Kentucky: A Guide to the Bluegrass State.* American Guide Series (New York, 1939).

would be in the interior close to the principal entrances, but most sites would be along the 300 miles of shoreline. Considerations of access and administration suggested that they be clustered at the north, south, and near the center at Golden Pond; but there was no early attempt to assign precise locations or to make detailed layouts in a master plan.

Rather, primarily attention was addressed to the question: Why do American families camp? This question was put to organizations of family campers and to individual families who had experience in camping. The first torrent of answers gradually clarified to reflect a picture of camping as a kind of shorthand used to describe a variety of outdoor recreation activities, only a few of which were being served by existing campgrounds in federal recreation areas.

People, it seems, camp for a variety of reasons: Some families camp to save money—the choice between two weeks of camping or a few days in motels or a beach cottage. Other families camp as a basis for pursuing a favorite outdoor hobby—fishing, boating, hiking, hunting, swimming, sightseeing, birdwatching, or just enjoying the fresh air. To complicate the planners' problems, different members of the same family often wished to pursue different hobbies at the same camp at the same time. For a small but growing number of gadgeteers, camping is an opportunity to use many homemade devices for campcraft and woodcraft.

Few of these reasons for camping require that the campground be located halfway across the continent in a national park or monument set aside to preserve superlative scenic or wilderness values. Any reasonably natural wooded site accessible to water will serve. The closer to home the more time can be spent in camp and less on crowded highways.

The planners of Land Between the Lakes also went to the trade associations representing the growing market for outdoor recreation equipment—tents, trailers, cots, mattresses, camping stoves, trailer boats, water skis. "What kind of camping facilities," they asked, "are the people who buy your equipment looking for?" The trailer people provided specific answers. First, they said, are roadside camps suitable for an overnight stand en route to some further destination. Second are weekend camps attractive enough to draw the family for a couple of days away from home. Third are camps in metropolitan areas specifically intended to provide low-cost accommodations for families who are sightseeing in the big cities, or attending a world's fair, convention, or other special event. Finally are destination camps intended to attract and hold a vacationing family for a week or more during their vacation.

Armed with this information, TVA concluded that the design of a public campground could not remain, as it had long been, a designer's stepchild. Obviously, the problem would not disappear if ignored long enough. Nor could it be tucked into an out-of-the-way corner. Rather, the approach had to be a positive one responsive to the varied needs and demands of the camping public, yet recognizing the limitations of many variables, such as site, space, weather, and geography.

The design of the Rushing Creek Campground, the first in Land Between the Lakes, reflected many concepts then novel in campground design. Hot and cold showers and flush toilets replaced the pit privies and trench latrines which have so long symbolized camping to the American public. The camper had his own waterfront for his use. He did not have to contend with crowds of weekend and day users. Rustic materials such as logs and stones were replaced by colorful panels and frames (originally developed for industrial use) which were easy to keep clean.

With some trepidation TVA announced the opening of the Rushing Creek Campground to the public on June 1, 1964, only sixty days after groundbreaking. The first campers, a father and son from Indiana, arrived the evening before in order to be the first to try out this new camping experience. Campers, it seems, are "sidewalk superintendents," like most of the rest of the American public.

Chapter Seven

Innovations

TRANSLATION of the original concept into a program of family camping has continued since 1964, despite many pressures created by high land costs and other demands on the federal budget. The family campgrounds in Land Between the Lakes offer innovations that continue to draw many plaudits and few complaints.

These innovations include:

1. A method of operation that basically treats a campground as a motel. Campsites, like motel rooms, are "a home away from home"—one's private castle during the period of his occupancy. Roads, paths, toilets, beaches, launching ramps, playfields, amphitheaters, hiking trails, and all activities within the campground are for the camper and other campground guests, not for the general public. In short, the camper in Land Between the Lakes, while he is there, is a member of a camping community—a community of common interests, not one of a minority among a heterogeneous group.

2. In Land Between the Lakes the gates of the campground close when it reaches planned capacity. There are no overlapping tent ropes, no overcrowding in the family campgrounds.

3. Campgrounds in Land Between the Lakes are equipped with the basic utilities that man has developed to provide a clean, safe, healthful, and sanitary environment and to reduce the number of waking hours that must be devoted to personal maintenance. To the purist these facilities may seem to be an unwarranted intrusion of the urban environment into the wild, but to those who have had the experience, they are recognized as indispensable aids to a pleasant time in the out-of-doors. Hours released from campground drudgery and freed from concern over safety and cleanliness all contribute to a memorable camping experience. As one husband put it when the family was

leaving, "This is the first time I have ever gotten my wife to come camping with me and the boys. Her only question now is how soon we can come again."

4. All campgrounds in Land Between the Lakes do not yet provide individual utility connections at each campsite. Once their basic concerns for safety and sanitation are satisfied, campers still prefer those sites which contain the highest degree of natural amenities, frequently expressed as "a little shade and a view of the water."

5. Nor do facilities and an attractive setting alone completely fill the camping picture. Under contract with neighboring universities in western Kentucky and southern Illinois, TVA has devised a work-learn experience employing senior and graduate students in the Land Between the Lakes campgrounds. These students are instructed in the art of a soft-sell approach designed to involve campers in a variety of campground activities. Nobody has to participate, but the students are there to help the novice with his equipment, to guide him along the nature trails, to supervise campground games and entertainment, and to be generally helpful.

Response to this program from both students and campers has been heartwarming. One student observed that he would have been glad to pay for his summer's experience rather than receive pay. This same student was sought out by parents who wanted to meet "the young man our children talk about all the time." Other campground guests have taken the time to write to express appreciation for their vacation experience in Land Between the Lakes. Seldom do these letters fail to compliment the personable young men and women who work in the campgrounds and who have contributed so much to the family's happy experience in Land Between the Lakes.

6. Early in the first camping season TVA was approached by the pastor of a local church who requested permission to hold church services in one of the campgrounds. From this request there has grown the Land Between the Lakes Area Ministry, an interdenominational group representing the religious denominations in the surrounding region. The Ministry's program, at TVA's insistence, provides not only preaching but a pastoral service throughout the summer months. Many campers appreciate the opportunity to worship in an informal atmosphere. They also enjoy the security of knowing that pastoral services are at hand in the event of an emergency.

Not all family camping needs are met in the large and fully staffed and equipped campgrounds. Many camping families prefer more isolated locations and have learned to do with fewer of the accouterments of civilization. They have learned how to do with less and what to leave at home. The reward for traveling light is that they can sometimes get closer to a favorite fishing spot or section of lakeshore. For this group TVA, in turn, does not have to worry about winterproofing water supplies. Chemical toilets will suffice, and the camper can bring his own water sufficient for overnight or a weekend. For these families Land Between the Lakes provides a score or more of lake access areas available for both camping and picnicking. Each area is equipped with tables, garbage and cleanup services, access roads, parking areas, boat launching ramps, and chemical toilets. A few afford drinking water. Unlike the larger family campgrounds, they may be used throughout the year, but they do not provide for the community activities available in the larger campgrounds during the summer season.

Early in the development of Land Between the Lakes, TVA received a letter from the wife of a professor. She wrote, "I have been following reports of camping areas in Land Between the Lakes with interest . . . I do hope that areas will be set aside for primitive camping . . . areas as close to natural as possible . . . where families who enjoy wilder areas [may camp] without competing with . . . houses on wheels." This concerned citizen was assured that among the 170,000 acres of Land Between the Lakes campsites would be designated to meet her wishes.

The family camping program in Land Between the Lakes continues to evolve with many prospects in varying degrees of fulfillment. The first year-round camp—Piney, near Fort Henry—was opened in July 1969. All its utilities are winterized so that campers may use it throughout the year. It remains to be seen, however, whether campers will come in sufficient numbers to justify the personnel necessary for the camp's year-round operation. The experience to date shows that campgrounds will be overcrowded during June, July, and August but will attract only a handful of families during the remainder of the year. Much of the best of the camping season goes unused—the spring crappie run, the burgeoning growth of spring, and the glories of autumn color, not to mention the harvest moon. A very considerable investment for which the taxpayers have paid lies idle. The only sound explanation for this phenomenon lies in the habits of past generations which tie vacation time to the summer months when children are out of school.

Other developing facets of the program demonstrate the early need for a family campground on Lake Barkley, a campground designed to take advantage of the differing characteristics of the two lakes, Barkley and Kentucky. This campground will be oriented to the needs of sportsmen—fishing and hunting—for which Lake Barkley is admirably suited. The campgrounds on Kentucky Lake then can be oriented more directly to those activities known as "water contact sports"—swimming, boating, water skiing, scuba diving, and the others.

The program envisions overnight camping facilities for those who wish to explore the interior of Land Between the Lakes on horseback, afoot, or by trailmobile. Plans also visualize something known as an "air camp" for the growing number of American families who measure the radius of their weekend and vacation territory not by the miles of their car's odometer but by the air miles logged in their private plane. The problems of the air campers are uniquely different from those of the earthbound camper, even though the need for special assistance to this type of recreationist is by no means as great.

A final facet of the camping program in Land Between the Lakes is the question of camper services. The basic concept of Land Between the Lakes is that it be uncluttered by evidences of commercial activities which are essentially part of the urban scene. Land Between the Lakes is intended always to remain essentially as open space, equipped with only the minimum of facilities and services essential for the user's health, safety, convenience, and enjoyment. The gamut of commercial services which has sprung up to serve America's leisure needs are left behind as one crosses the bridges into Land Between the Lakes.

This idea, however, presents some troublesome problems. "Why," the camper asks, "should I have to take an hour or more out of my day to run into town to get milk for the children or marine gas for the boat?" Another asks, "If you expect me to bring all the family's food for a week, why don't you at least provide a place where I can buy ice to keep it?" The problem becomes how to answer them without opening the door to the entire roster of services and supplies under conditions which would immediately re-create the urban environment from which Land Between the Lakes is designed to be a temporary escape. Solutions lie, perhaps, in such devices as a rolling store, coin-operated concessions, or even floating stores. These will be studied and may, when crowds are sufficient, have to be admitted. Meanwhile there is a wide variety of camper supplies in the immediately surrounding areas.

Organized camping has long been an accepted part of the American culture. Yet today camping authorities estimate that from 75 to 80 percent of all children in the United States (age 6 to 16) have never camped. Each summer finds no more than 10 percent of American children in camp. Translated into numbers, this means that between 35 and 40 million American children will reach adulthood without having had a camping experience. All this is despite the fact that across the United States five million children camp each summer in more than 15,000 camping establishments operated by public, voluntary, and private agencies. Publicly operated camps form only a small minority, 2 percent of the resident camps and 10 percent of day camps.

Students of camping bring out other interesting data. Ninety-eight percent of all group camping occurs during two months, July and August. Ninety-six percent of all campers come from urban areas. The concentration of both camp patrons and camp facilities is highest in the industrial Northeast; it is lowest in the South. Most campers come from either the upper income bracket or from the lower brackets. In this case children from the middle income groups are the under-privileged. Wealthy families can send their children to one of a wide variety of camps catering to almost any whim or special interest from outdoor sports to fine arts. Children from low income brackets may be the beneficiaries of a camping experience subsidized by a civic club or a welfare group. Families in between, however, can neither afford to send their children to camp nor qualify for aid from welfare groups.

Land Between the Lakes can contribute to organized camping in many ways. Among these are:

1. To introduce camping facilities into at least a corner of the urbanizing South while at the same time staying within reach of mid-America.

2. To try to reach children from all income levels.

3. To break the seasonal barrier by providing camping facilities in months other than July and August.

4. To experiment in an area which has become encrusted with tradition and not subject to the stimulation of the marketplace.

The planners of Land Between the Lakes made certain basic assumptions to guide their thinking about a camping program for organized groups. These are:

1. That all camping programs will be "demonstration oriented." Every opportunity will be sought to experiment with new kinds of

camp facilities, new kinds of camp activities, and various forms of camp organization.

2. That most camp facilities will be winterized so that group camping can be conducted on a year-round basis.

3. That the total area of Land Between the Lakes (170,000 acres) will be available for use by group campers as a resource for camping programs and activities.

4. That the camps will provide the opportunity for groups to conduct new and different kinds of programs. The mere duplication of typical camp programs and facilities found elsewhere will be avoided.

5. That effective camping must place its emphasis on programs related to education as well as to recreation and entertainment.

These assumptions were placed before a consulting team assembled by Milton A. Gabrielsen of New York University with a request that it study group camping opportunities in Land Between the Lakes. The resulting report[1] outlined five basic types of group camp programs which the study team believes are possibilities for Land Between the Lakes. These are 1) outdoor education and school camping, 2) leadership training, 3) primitive camping, 4) summer group camping, and 5) experimental camping.

OUTDOOR EDUCATION AND SCHOOL CAMPING

It was not difficult for TVA to select the educational field for early emphasis in the camping programs for organized groups in Land Between the Lakes. In many respects TVA is an education agency, experienced in the fields of conservation and development of natural resources.

Outdoor recreation is not the same as outdoor education. TVA was forcibly reminded of this by professionals in both fields and readily accepted it. The school camping center of Land Between the Lakes thus became a part of its Conservation Education Center.

The philosophy undergirding outdoor education has been well stated by L. B. Sharp, patron saint of the outdoor educators. "That which can best be learned inside the classroom should be learned there. That

[1] New York University, School of Education Consultants, *Report on Organized Group Camp Centers* (New York, July 15, 1964).

which can best be learned in the out-of-doors through direct experience dealing with native materials and life situations should there be learned."[2] Despite its logic and the lip service paid to Dr. Sharp's philosophy, however, few school systems of the nation practice it. Educators still try to carry on too much of the educational process within the confines of brick and mortar.

Characteristically, the Land Between the Lakes administrators sought to learn why; and they were not satisfied with the answer, "It costs too much." It has long been an axiom that what the American people really want they are willing to pay for—highways, for example. In response to further questions, TVA was given more answers, frequently in the form of still different questions: "Parents will object. The children won't be safe. Teachers cannot be expected to supervise thirty children outside the classroom. Not all children have proper outdoor clothes and camping equipment. How will they be able to get proper food? Teachers are not prepared to be experts on all the subjects that will come up in an outdoor situation. Who will answer these ques-tions?"

The common thread running through all these answers and further questions boils down to only one: How can the classroom teacher feel secure while conducting an outdoor education experience for her thirty or more classroom charges? To provide a satisfactory answer to this single question, other questions had to be answered. Some of these are troublesome questions of cost, public liability, transportation, addi-tional supervision and teaching skills, and others relative to the same problems. The Land Between the Lakes staff itself could provide only some of the answers but was confident that, with the enthusiastic sup-port of concerned teachers, answers could be found in many communi-ties that would satisfy parents, taxpayers, and school administrators. Today Land Between the Lakes has provided its share of the answers. School systems in four surrounding states have also provided answers, several with the help of federal funds supplied under Title III of the Elementary and Secondary Education Act of 1965.

As part of their conservation education program, TVA has built the Youth Station, an outdoor school accommodating sixty pupils and an

[2] "Introduction," American Association for Health, Physical Education, and Recreation. *Outdoor Education for American Youth* (Washington, D. C., 1957).

adult leadership of twelve. The "schoolyard" is a fifty-acre peninsula extending into Lake Barkley and accessible only by causeway. The "schoolhouse" is a group of eight buildings—a kitchen-dining hall, a resource materials structure, and six dormitories. The area for field trips includes all of Land Between the Lakes and points of interest between it and home. The site of the school was selected to assure the teacher that she and her pupils would find a safe and secure setting for their pioneering week's activities in what for many would be a new and strange environment, the out-of-doors. She need not fear for the safety of the children from unforeseen hazards that might exist in an area not already explored by trained educators.

Two thoughts furnished the primary guides to the design of the kitchen-dining room. To the concern for the safety and security of the teacher and her pupils was added the concern of educators that outdoor curricula too frequently are slaves to the kitchen schedule. "In outdoor situations," TVA was told, "the business of learning plays second fiddle to the business of eating." It might have been said, "The cook speaks louder than the teacher."

It was important to find a way that classes in the Youth Station could be served appetizing and nutritious meals in ways and at times that would not warp the learning process. The answer came in a special line of prepared quick-frozen meals developed for TVA by one of the nation's largest food processors. Their work was based on research performed under contract with Michigan State University and New York University. The kitchen-dining room is designed around this special line of prepared frozen meals. A meal for the entire student body and its leaders can be put on the table by one or two people on as little as thirty minutes' notice. The kitchen is noteworthy for the size of its electric freezer and refrigeration facilities and for the ovens in which the frozen meals are brought quickly to serving temperatures. It is even more noteworthy for its lack of conventional equipment, such as potato peelers, cabbage shredders, and dishwashers. All table utensils are disposable, made of paper, aluminum foil, or plastic. Without kitchen chores, camp personnel are free between meals to take on cleaning and other maintenance tasks—not to mention working with the pupils.

For the operators of the school, the Youth Station demonstrates low on-site labor costs and, indeed, overcomes much of the difficulty in obtaining any labor at all at remote locations. For the program director the days' activities can be planned free of the restrictions imposed by a rigid dining room schedule. No longer does a bugle sound or a bell ring to announce a seven o'clock breakfast or dinner at noon. The educational program can now call for birdwatching at sunrise, a mid-day hike, or an early supper before an evening's visit to a deer lick without any difficulty.

The resource materials building is a multipurpose structure combining library and laboratory facilities with shelter space for use when inclement weather forces classes indoors. Such emergencies are rare, however, for many of the best educational experiences are found in rain and snow. From the resource materials building classes and individuals may draw fishing gear, boots, small animal traps, telescopes, field glasses, microscopes, books, and other supplies and equipment needed in outdoor studies.

The six dormitories are identical in design but are scattered informally along the contours of a wooded ridge. Each will accommodate eight to twelve youngsters and two teachers or adult counselors, who also assist in supervision and informal instruction. The counselors usually come from the home community where they are recruited from among parents, retired teachers, college and high school students, and other community leaders willing to contribute their time.

The Youth Station is intended to serve children in the fourth through the ninth grades. Younger than this, children are not prepared to benefit from a resident outdoor educational experience. Beyond the ninth grade, schools become involved in problems of conflicting schedules arising from specialized lines of study. Because of the variations in age and the differing needs of individual schools, the staff of Land Between the Lakes does not prepare a fixed schedule of activities to be followed by all groups using the Youth Station. Instead, the small staff has prepared a series of educational stations and program guides. With these and an occasional helping hand, the teacher, hopefully with the full participation of her pupils and other adult counselors, plans a program to suit the needs and capabilities of her group.

As a part of the conservation education program the Youth Station is one of the most effective tools for teaching young people conservation and man's dependence on the natural environment. A school need not narrowly limit its outdoor curriculum to conservation subjects while at the Youth Station. The outdoors is an admirable setting in which to study art, crafts, English composition, mathematics, the life sciences, and a host of other subjects.

The first years were very rewarding in terms of the kinds of school use which prevailed within the conservation education programs. The Youth Station, being the focal point of all school activity, has been well received by the local and regional schools. During the first school year's use, beginning May 1966 and ending April 1967, twenty-two schools used the facilities. The second year showed a marked increase; fifty-seven schools came from as far away as 300 miles. Now the Youth Station is regularly booked at nearly full capacity.

The Youth Station has been a multiple-use facility. It not only has accommodated its intended use by school groups in the conservation education phase of the school program but also has doubled in brass as a facility for teacher training in the field. Training has been provided for both the preservice and in-service teacher. Several of the colleges and universities in the surrounding area have made use of the Conservation Education Center area for purposes of training the preservice teacher. Schools such as Murray State University, Southern Illinois University, Indiana University, Lambuth College, Memphis State University, Texas A. & M. University, University of Tennessee, and others have used the facility to broaden the education of undergraduates and to lend greater insight into the area of conservation education for graduate students.

The Elementary and Secondary Education Act of 1965 has played an important role in outdoor and conservation education. Title III of this law authorizes funds for exemplary and innovative programs. Imaginative teachers have used these funds to finance or help finance such activities as resident outdoor school programs, away from home and schoolroom. Many of the schools which have come to Land Between the Lakes for resident programs have received Title III funds. Other parts of the Act have made it possible for local school systems to experiment with programs for the educationally and culturally deprived. Head Start, Upward Bound, and other educational enrichment programs have also found a need to include outdoor education within the program structure. All of these have been accommodated, from time to time, in the Youth Station.

In addition, the Conservation Education Center and its staff have played an important role in a new and fascinating project of the United

States Department of the Interior, National Park Service, program entitled National, Environmental Education Development (NEED). Education has long been claimed as a primary benefit of national parks, but little has been done to realize educational possibilities. Recently it has been recognized that environmental education must become a vital part of our national parks.

The National Park Service asked Mario M. Menesini of the University of California to prepare an environmental education program which could be used on a nationwide scale. His recommendation has fully utilized the experience of Land Between the Lakes. The program will be built in three phases. The first portion, geared to the elementary school level, will be projected toward developing a sense of awareness in the student. Phase two will incorporate the junior high level and deal with specific conservation practices and issues. The third phase will incorporate the high school level and will identify problematic situations of legislating on conservation matters. The Park Service also plans a program for day-use of school groups on areas which they will call environmental study areas. Background information will be provided to the schools concerning the natural, cultural, and historical significance of this specific site. Lessons being learned in Land Between the Lakes are thus being incorporated in new educational programs throughout the national park system.

The impact on pupils of a week at the Youth Station in Land Between the Lakes normally leads the local school administrators to two important conclusions: 1) An outdoor program is a must within the regular school curriculum; it does not function as extracurricular activity. 2) The facilities in Land Between the Lakes are not large enough or close enough to support a program for all of those whom they would like to participate. From this point the school must make an important decision: whether to obtain an area and provide facilities making possible a significant outdoor education program within their school system.

There is no simple solution to the problems which face all the various schools who wish to establish outdoor education programs. As a school identifies its own core of problems, it will find levels of difficulty which do not lead to easy remedies. The demand for such enrichment programs as outdoor education will create demand from within the framework of the school staff and from without in the form of parents and civic organizations. Outdoor or conservation education thus becomes a challenge. It is a challenge to local school administrators to find the time for such programs; a challenge to the states to exercise their authority and responsibility to lead in the development of progressive educational endeavors; a challenge to the parents who at times must participate and lend full backing; and last, a challenge to the teachers who in turn must challenge the students. Land Between the Lakes provides a demonstration, an opportunity for numerous school systems to experiment. But the individual school system must clearly bear the responsibility for establishing and meeting its own needs.

CAMPING CENTERS FOR SMALL GROUPS

One of the great needs in organized camping in the United States is a place where a small group of people, ranging in size from a station wagon load to a busload, may camp together safely and enjoyably. Some may wish to participate only in traditional forms of camping but the same location could also introduce them to new camping opportunities.

TVA's consultants pointed out that literally thousands of agencies in the United States representing churches, civic clubs, fraternal bodies, municipal recreation departments, voluntary youth-serving agencies, health groups, and many others would like to provide camping experiences for their own members or for others in their community. Most are prevented from doing so because of the prohibitive costs of acquiring and maintaining suitable land and camp facilities. Others have their impulse to serve in this way blunted by the frustrations of meeting adequate standards of health and sanitation. Still others have the desire but lack the know-how. Land Between the Lakes provided the opportunity to develop one or more small group camping centers that could become the means of opening up new vistas of camping for thousands of children and adults who otherwise would never have the opportunity.

The image of the frontier hero striking into the woods and carrying the means of meeting all his physical needs on his back is a part of the cultural heritage of every American boy. Today's parents, however, insist that today's camping frontier be cleaned up, sanitized, and made safe. If they did not so insist, health officers, educators, and other people undertaking the responsibility of camping would do so.

More than any other one factor, this insistence on modern facilities for health and sanitation has increased the cost of camping in organized groups. No longer is it possible to pass the hat at a civic luncheon or sell candy around the neighborhood to raise funds to send a few boys off for a week in the out-of-doors. Needed are centers capable of accommodating groups of various sizes from six to sixty. These centers should be equipped with toilets, shelters, beds, and kitchens. This camp must be supervised by a staff more skilled than most parents and adults in taking children into the out-of-doors. Since such a camp will be used by more than one group at a time, the leadership must be skilled in directing the sharing of common space and activities with members of other groups, probably from different communities, different races, and different ethnic backgrounds.

As the responsible proprietor and landlord for such a camp, TVA is in the process of establishing ground rules governing length of stay, liability, safety, and the use and operation of the equipment provided. All of this will have to be done at the lowest possible cost. But it will provide a public service now largely unmet for most of our urban areas.

For these reasons the construction of camping centers for small groups was given high priority, following outdoor education and school camping. One such center has been completed, and a second is on the drafting boards. In July of 1968 TVA opened Camp Energy for year-round use. Energy was named for a community which once existed near its site—one that had disappeared long before Land Between the Lakes came into being. With a total capacity of 400, Camp Energy accommodates groups of any size from six upwards to its full capacity. Its winterized toilets, drinking water, picnic tables, and campsites are so arranged that small groups will have a degree of privacy and yet be able to join with others in common activities. Camp Energy is close to the Conservation Education Center with its array of educational stations to be used by groups both large and small.

A nearby bivouac area can accommodate groups of up to 500 or more persons. This has been designed for the experienced camper. In the bivouac area the group can be on its own if it wishes, but within the area TVA has provided toilets, a safe water supply, and a field kitchen complete with electric outlets. Accessible to a seventeen-mile hiking trail, back roads for horseback riding, Energy Lake for quiet water sports, and a dozen or so miles of lakeshore, the bivouac area is an ideal location for Scout jamborees, for groups of hunters, and for others who are skilled in the camping arts.

73

Neither Camp Energy nor its related bivouac area provides a dining hall and bunks. Groups must bring their own shelter and sleeping gear in the form of tents, trailers, or sleeping bags. Each group must bring its own food and be ready to prepare it. Thus Camp Energy does not fully meet the prescription laid down by the consultants for Land Between the Lakes. Rather, it represents a situation where lack of funds to build dormitories and dining rooms had produced from an inventive staff a new and unique kind of camping facility. With adequate leadership this kind of facility may safely bring novice campers even closer to nature than would be possible in a conventional camp.

On the basis of limited experience, TVA has found that it is not enough simply to provide the facility. Neither is it enough to prepare and hand out colorful brochures describing it. Without a thoroughly planned program of promotion, Camp Energy will remain an undiscovered jewel. Accordingly, intensive efforts are made to inform agencies and nearby communities about Camp Energy and its potentialities as one of the features of Land Between the Lakes. These efforts include contacts by telephone or in person with the national, regional, state, and local agencies representing the Boy and Girl Scouts, 4-H clubs, churches, settlement and neighborhood houses, and a host of others. The purpose is to familiarize these groups with Camp Energy and with Land Between the Lakes so that they can describe it to their own members in terms of their own programs and interests.

Still on the drafting boards are plans for a second camping center for small groups. Brandon Spring Camp is designed for groups of visitors to remain in residence for periods of one to two weeks. The groups will include children and adults from various educational, conservation, religious, outdoor, community, and service organizations. Among its users are expected to be classes from junior high and high schools; school bands, choruses, and ball teams; teachers and parents; handicapped and aging persons; sportsmen; and other groups interested in the out-of-doors. From Brandon Spring Camp as a base, these groups will use and enjoy many or all of the various outdoor recreation and conservation education opportunities in Land Between the Lakes.

The Brandon Spring Camp is being designed to contain housing accommodations and feeding facilities for a maximum of 250 people. Like Camp Energy, it can accommodate groups of varying sizes from a single station wagon load up to the maximum. Special attention is being given to flexibility of food service, sanitation, and safety features.

Compact design will minimize the impact on the natural features of the site. Because these features require the major capital investment and because experience in Land Between the Lakes has shown that it does not cost proportionately more to winterize water supply and toilet facilities, all these features will be designed and built for winter as well as summer use.

The Brandon Spring Camp will be ready to serve a great variety of groups having a great variety of interests. Brandon Spring is expected to fulfill many of the educational purposes provided for in the Conservation Education Center at the opposite end of Land Between the Lakes.

PRIMITIVE CAMPING

French and English traders of the seventeenth and early eighteenth centuries were, of course, the first Europeans to practice primitive camping in Land Between the Lakes. They found what is known today as primitive camping to be a way of life among its Indian occupants. Primitive camping is practiced today in Land Between the Lakes by hunters, fishermen, and families along its trails and lakeshore and as "outpost" camping from the Youth Station and by troops of Boy and Girl Scouts. As more facilities for groups are provided, primitive camping will increase among organizations of young people under adult supervision.

Facilities for primitive camping are relatively simple and inexpensive. What is required is a staff of responsible people adequately trained and organized to assure that the areas open to camping are safe, healthful, and secure. This staff also serves as a backup to the leaders of the visiting groups to provide information, inspiration, and emergency help. The Land Between the Lakes organization supplies all of these in addition to the terrain and trails.

DEMONSTRATION CAMP FOR LARGE GROUPS

TVA foresees the time when it will provide camp facilities in Land Between the Lakes where large groups can experiment and gain experience with new and different kinds of camping programs. Recently one of the communities neighboring Land Between the Lakes has experimented with camping programs as a means of reaching potential dropouts among junior high and high school students. The community had set up an excellent program using one of its downtown school buildings. Experience in this program led some of its teachers to believe that a camping experience would provide a highly effective tool for reaching some of the enrollees. They arranged to bring a group to the Youth Station in Land Between the Lakes. Among this group were students who had never known an environment other than their own household, the schoolroom, and the streets between. A sizable proportion had never been far enough into a forest to be out of the sight of buildings. A few days' exposure to such objects as a deer skeleton and a snapping turtle in hibernation provided a whole new frame of reference which the educators find to be a powerful stimulus and incentive to learning.

The opportunity to take his student body into a resident camp provides the urban school administrator with at least two important tools for dealing with the physical and emotional restlessness of today's urban youth that the schoolground simply cannot provide. These are an exposure of our youth to the natural landscape and twenty-four-hour living situation with persons other than those in the immediate family. A camp, capable of accommodating up to 250 or 300 persons, will offer not only educators but those responsible for healing various physical and mental health problems new opportunities for reaching people.

Outdoor settings away from urban distractions provide a superior locale for specialized training in music, sports, the arts, aquatics, reading, and science. The camp environment is favorable for meeting the special needs of the physically handicapped, the emotionally disturbed, the mentally retarded, and the victims of various other health problems. Participation in an organized group sharing a common problem and under adequate supervision is often the best way of introducing the individual to a whole new world outside his own narrow and frequently warped environment. Families interested in camping but equipped with neither the know-how nor the means to undertake it may find participation in a supervised program for other novice family campers an introduction to the out-of-doors that would not otherwise be within their reach. In Land Between the Lakes TVA can provide not only the locale and the facilities for an almost infinite variety of camping programs but also a specialized staff which can work with educational agencies in helping to develop new values in camping.

Chapter Eight

Wildlife Management

THERE IS a long history of close cooperation between TVA and the United States Fish and Wildlife Service. In fact, in the 1940s TVA had conveyed to the Service for use as a part of Kentucky Woodlands several thousand acres of land acquired in connection with Kentucky Reservoir. Refuge boundaries have long been shown on all plans for recreation development of Kentucky Reservoir, for they enclosed many miles of its most scenic lakeshore. Walter Gresh, former director of the Southeastern Region of the United States Fish and Wildlife Service, was the first person outside TVA with whom TVA staff discussed its concept of Land Between the Lakes. On this occasion Gresh listened with growing enthusiasm, added some of his own thoughts, and finally commented, "The only thing wrong with your idea is that we didn't think of it first!"

The space available for wildlife management in the Kentucky Woodlands in 1964 was about 60,000 acres. Under TVA's concept of multiple-use administration, Land Between the Lakes would provide 170,000 acres—nearly a threefold increase. In addition to the waterfowl management program in Land Between the Lakes, the authorization for the Barkley Project stipulated replacement of the Kentucky Woodlands' waterfowl features upstream on Lake Barkley in Stewart County, Tennessee, but outside the boundaries of Land Between the Lakes. Much of the newly acquired acreage in Land Between the Lakes is in a condition more desirable for upland species than the former refuge land.

Although surrounded by three hundred miles of lakeshore fronting on two of the largest impounded lakes in the world, Land Between the Lakes lacks natural interior waters. It has almost no year-round free-

flowing streams, few ponds. Moreover, many of the springs for which
the area was known have in modern times been submerged by the
waters of either Kentucky Lake or Lake Barkley. Others of which the
area is reputed to have boasted in earlier times have either dried up
as the result of poor land management in private hands or existed only
in the minds of the region's promoters. To help remedy this lack of
interior water a ninety-acre lake, Hematite, had been built in the late
1930s as a federal work-relief project. To Hematite, TVA set to work
to add three other sizable subimpoundments within the Lake Barkley
basin. If built at all within reasonable cost limits, the dams to create
these subimpoundments had to be completed ahead of the rising
waters of Lake Barkley, scheduled finally in the summer of 1966.
Accordingly, among the earliest developmental efforts that TVA undertook was the building of dams creating Honker Lake, 190 acres; Energy
Lake, 370 acres; and Bards Lake, 320 acres. All serve as multipurpose
lakes, benefiting both wildlife and recreation interests. They add to
the aesthetics of the area by permanently submerging creek bottoms
that would otherwise be periodically exposed as mud flats during periods
of summer drawdown. They provide educational and recreation opportunities not available on the broad expanses and sometimes rough
water of the larger lakes. They are used by fishermen and provide a
safe haven for small boats and canoes. They provide feeding and
resting areas for waterfowl. Portions of their shorelines afford superior
locations for campgrounds.

Land Between the Lakes is an area of low relief. Its climax vegetation
is hardwood forest. Unless the forest is cleared in places, a visit to the
region can become a visit to a land of no horizons, no vistas, to a land
between the trees—not Land Between the Lakes. To learn this, one
has only to experience the relative monotony of some of the land once
cleared but now reverted to forest in the former Woodlands Refuge.
In pleasant contrast, the open meadows and hillsides still reflect the
former pattern of farms north and south of the refuge. To be sure,
many of these have become ugly through the forces of erosion and
mismanagement, but replacement of their openness with solid forest is
not a good answer. Unfortunately, to those early charged with management of the refuge lands, return to forest appears to have been the
only alternative to eroding fields.

So the planners of Land Between the Lakes saw in the long sweeps
of utility lines that crossed it the opportunity to maintain, and to create,

vistas. They knew also that the richest habitat for upland wildlife is not the central forest but the forest margin. Every mile of transmission line through a forested area creates two miles of forest margin, one on either side. The unyielding double, straight edge bounding the shortest distance between two points is "unnatural" as are the vertical forest walls marching uniformly to the horizon. But when one controls the adjoining land as well as the right-of-way, these forest edges can be varied both horizontally and vertically. This can be accomplished over a period of years and at no great expense by minor modifications of forest management plans and by appropriate management of the right-of-way itself.

Work was begun on a ten-mile stretch of electric transmission line that crossed a portion of the Conservation Education Center and has since been extended to a similar section of a heavier line. Funds that would normally be spent on routine herbicidal treatment are matched by Land Between the Lakes funds and are used instead to plow away undesirable growth, prepare the ground, fertilize and reseed with food and cover plantings for wildlife. At highway crossings, along hiking and horseback trails, and at other places frequented by the public, care is also taken to plant species that return aesthetic as well as wildlife benefits in the form of spring flowers, autumn color, or winter green.

A similar activity has been carried on within Land Between the Lakes by the private operators of a natural gas transmission line that crosses the area. Under the terms of the license agreement providing for "looping" of an existing line, the Michigan-Wisconsin Gas Transmission Line Company has revegetated construction scars and provides an annual maintenance program that has enriched the value of the right-of-way for wildlife, particularly deer and wild turkey. Specifically, the company used a mixture of legumes and grasses that wildlife find much more palatable than the usual fescue. Consciously or not, the company is here demonstrating a tangible act of industrial statesmanship and resource husbandry that might well be emulated elsewhere.

Three other tools of land management are being employed for the benefit of wildlife in Land Between the Lakes. All three will also return aesthetic benefits, will enhance the environment for outdoor recreation by helping to maintain a pleasing balance between field and forest. The first is to create woods openings and waterholes throughout the forested area. The second is to create groves of evergreens within the prevailing hardwoods. The third is to maintain appropriate acreages in cropland, pasture, and brush rather than plant trees or allow the land to revert to forest.

The size of the home range required by a given species of wildlife is determined by the availability of food, water, cover, and living space. A forest cast with frequent small openings of grass, herbs, and brush provides a better environment for most species than one whose mantle of trees is unbroken. If these forest openings are blessed with water, so much the better!

Management plans for Land Between the Lakes contain provision for creating or maintaining woods openings and waterholes at about half-mile intervals throughout its forested areas—more than 250 in all. These openings will vary from ridge crest to slope to creek bottom. Some will be visible from roads where the game they attract may be easily viewed by the motorist, but most will be at remote locations best known to the deer, turkey, rabbits, quail, and other wild creatures for whose delight they are intended.

A second means of introducing variety and richness to the wildlife habitat of Land Between the Lakes is the planting of groves of evergreens at intervals throughout the hardwood forest. In all, nearly three hundred of these groves of pine or cedar are projected. Like forest openings, these will average five acres in size and will be located at about one-half-mile intervals. Twenty percent of these plantings have been completed, and more will follow to provide midday and midwinter shelter for deer, turkey, and other wildlife.

About 15 or 20 percent of Land Between the Lakes will be maintained as cropland and pasture to grow food for wildlife and to add variety to the landscape. Old farms in upper creek bottoms and gentle hillsides are ideal for this purpose, although so are the long sweeps of utility rights-of-way.

Farming is a widely accepted tool in management of both waterfowl and upland game. Corn, soy beans, and milo are favorite foods for the skeins and wedges of wild geese that arrive each autumn. If an area can be flooded when the crop is ripe, millet and buckwheat are preferred. Geese also like a salad in the form of ladino clover, ryegrass, wheat, or barley. Favored locations include creek bottoms, particularly those above Energy and Hematite lakes. Others lie along Cravens Creek, Duncan Creek, and Smith Creek in the north and Bear Creek in the south. At places where fall drawdown exposes expanses of the former bottomlands bordering the Cumberland and Tennessee rivers themselves, Land Between the Lakes' wildlife managers can sometimes grow a quick crop right at the water's edge. This is handy for geese and ducks but involves the risk, for the manager and the taxpayer, that the investment of time and money may fall prey to the rising waters of an unseasonable flood.

Farm operations in Land Between the Lakes are carried out in part by TVA's own staff, a practice known in the construction industry as "force account." By this method 100 percent of the crop raised reaches its intended consumer—waterfowl, deer, turkey, and other species of wildlife. A second method, on a sharecropping basis, employs farmers from the surrounding area who, by agreement, expand operations on their home farms to designated acreages in Land Between the Lakes. These farmers are licensed to carry out certain farming practices that will provide wildlife and aesthetic benefits for Land Between the Lakes. Their pay is a share of the crops they raise, usually 75 percent. By this method, only 25 percent of the crop is left for wildlife, but this share is paid for by services rendered, not dollars from the taxpayers' pockets. Both methods have their advantages and disadvantages. The appropriate method is selected on whichever basis promises to return the greater benefit to the public.

No matter what is done in Land Between the Lakes to attract migratory waterfowl, the numbers that winter there are determined by factors over which TVA has no control. In recent years draining of wetlands and sustained draughts in northern Minnesota, the Dakotas, and Canada have severely restricted available breeding grounds. Wintering grounds in states to the north of Land Between the Lakes "shortstop" many geese or ducks, just as the effort in the Tennessee Valley tends to hold them away from latitudes still farther south. Those that do reach the latitudes of Land Between the Lakes find their choice no longer restricted to the offerings of the former Kentucky Woodlands Wildlife Refuge.

In recent years the states, as well as the United States Fish and Wildlife Service, have acquired substantial acreages along the inland rivers that attract thousands of ducks and geese. Better farming practices, including literally thousands of farm ponds, also join in the competition for the dwindling numbers of migrants that annually trek southward from northern breeding areas.

The decline of waterfowl in migration has heightened public interest in resident flocks. In Land Between the Lakes the wildlife management staff is directing its efforts toward developing and maintaining resident flocks of wood ducks, mallards, and Canada geese. Wood ducks nest in the area. Although they prefer hollow trees, there are not always enough at locations protected from predators, such as raccoons, which regard wood duck eggs as gourmet items. TVA is providing wood duck boxes, protected against predators. Similar efforts are being made with respect to mallards. Some success has come in developing a resident flock of Canada geese, one that will remain throughout the year within fifty to sixty miles of their home base on Honker Lake.

Land Between the Lakes boasts the only remaining native flock of wild turkey in the Commonwealth of Kentucky and one of the very few remaining in the East. For this we must thank two brothers, Shelley and James Nickell, themselves descendants of one of the first European families to settle "between the rivers." Once abundant in the virgin hardwood timber covering the broad ridges between the Tennessee and the Cumberland, wild turkeys at the turn of the century had been reduced by hunting, poaching, timber cutting, fire, and land clearing to a remnant flock of only eight birds on the Nickell Farm. Instilled with respect for these majestic birds, James and Shelley took steps to protect them in a remote section of their father's 800-acre farm. From 1900 to 1912, they watched the size of the flock slowly increase but realized that their efforts alone might not be enough to ensure their survival. About then Shelley was deputized by the Common-wealth of Kentucky as a volunteer state game warden, who then authorized protective measure for the birds. Public protection has continued ever since under state and federal auspices. Through the years birds have been trapped to restock other areas in Kentucky until in recent years it is believed that several thousand birds range through parts of twenty-three counties—all tracing their origin to the eight birds saved from extinction by the Nickell brothers in Land Between the Lakes.

Today perhaps 500 birds comprise the wild turkey community in Land Between the Lakes. For the most part, these wary creatures shun the roads, campgrounds, picnic areas, and open fields frequented by man. They prefer the more remote areas and are intolerant of human activity, particularly around their nesting areas during the spring nest-ing season. Their keen eyesight enables them to spot potential enemies and to scurry unseen to cover. Occasionally, however, the lucky motorist will glimpse them along road shoulders and in nearby forest openings.

Spring hunting for gobblers is permitted only on a managed basis. Hunting hours are restricted to those between daylight and mid-morning, and the bag limit is one bird per hunter per season.

Although not an area primarily dedicated to preservation, Land Between the Lakes is being so managed that the present flock is expected to increase from today's 500 birds to perhaps 3,000. This goal is based on management studies that indicate the area can ulti-mately support one bird on each 50 acres of 150,000. To reach such numbers will require full use of such management techniques as pro-viding the woods openings already described, waterholes, and control of human activity around favored haunts during the nesting season.

As with wild turkey, proper management of the 170,000 acres of Land Between the Lakes can bring about healthy increases in the numbers of other wildlife species of primary interest to sportsmen. The goals, in round numbers, are: 6,000 deer—1 per 25 acres on 150,000 acres; 3,000 turkey—1 per 50 acres on 150,000 acres; 75,000 squirrel—1 per 2 acres on 150,000 acres; 6,600 quail—1 per 3 acres on 20,000 acres; 10,000 rabbit—1 per 2 acres on 20,000 acres; 25,000 ducks—Peak popu-lation; 15,000 geese—Peak population.

Little attention is given, few studies devoted to nongame species of wildlife—fish, birds, or mammals. To judge by the increasing tonnages of sunflower and other wild bird seeds dispensed in every supermarket, the American public is displaying a widespread interest in songbirds. Yet too little is known about how to "manage" them. Probably some amateurs have amassed a great deal of information, but little effort has been devoted to searching out, collating, and applying such information. What trees and shrubs should the home gardener plant to attract his favorite songbirds? What measures may the managers of park and recreation areas employ to satisfy the mounting interest of the public in "ways of the wild"? These and similar questions are being con-sidered in the Land Between the Lakes development.

Enjoyment of wildlife is inversely proportional to the degree of artificiality in which it is seen. Yet some measure of the artificial is implicit in any form of management. Land Between the Lakes manage-ment plans are based on the concept of trying to bring about harmony between men and nature—a concept which embraces man as a part of the total natural scene. Under this concept, a beginning is being made toward instilling and extending an appreciation of wildlife for all visitors.

Chapter Nine

Conservation Education

LAND BETWEEN THE LAKES hopes to provide even the most casual visitor with at least a five-minute exposure to some new conservation idea. Every visit of whatever length should provide the visitor with a quality experience, one that involves him in the out-of-doors. In Land Between the Lakes TVA sees "a unique outdoor classroom and laboratory for those who like to lace their outdoor recreation pursuits with an educational flavor, an area to which people will be invited to come and do as well as to come and look; where the urban dweller can renew and maintain his contact with the land, the forest, and wildlife in its natural habitat—factors which are ingrained in the American tradition but which could easily be lost in the rapid urbanization and industrialization of the American countryside."[1] The uniqueness of Land Between the Lakes lies in its very lack of uniqueness. There are literally millions of acres not unlike it throughout eastern United States and elsewhere in the world. Lessons learned here can be applied elsewhere. It is a better laboratory than other public areas set aside as parks, monuments, and reserves primarily to protect, restore, or preserve.

The national park system, for example, places emphasis on scenic and natural wonders, primitive or wilderness areas, and historic features. Within the system, and quite properly, a nation has preserved its geysers, hot springs, caverns, canyons, natural bridges, and virgin stands of redwood. Elsewhere in the system are vast acreages of mountainslope, glacier, or forest, remote and inaccessible, unyielding to man's puny efforts to tame and cultivate them. Other units of the national park system preserve Independence Hall, the Statue of Liberty, and various battlefields—places concerned with the people and events that have shaped the history of our country.

By its very nature, then, the policies of the national park system tend to focus on the extraordinary. Attention is directed to the area and the events of which it was a part. Management becomes preoccupied with measures to preserve, restore, or interpret. The greater the event, the more it, rather than the visitor, becomes the center of attention. As a result, a visit to a national park may be an uplifting and inspiring experience; but so is a visit to an art gallery, an evening at the symphony, or a performance of Shakespeare. The visitor remains a member of the audience—at best, moved and inspired; at worst, merely entertained. Seldom does he become involved; the plans and policies to preserve the unique features of the system leave no room for this.

The further result is that the educational or interpretive programs of the National Park Service treat the visitor as part of an audience before whom a performance is to be staged. Most visitors do not stay long, so the performance is studied to assure that "a brief period which may be at the visitor's disposal can be in part devoted to the greatest available features."[2] Under these circumstances the performance is designed to become a cram session. That it is successful in meeting this objective is evidenced by more and more visitors, shorter and shorter visits, to more and more national parks. Increasingly, however, the National Park Service is disturbed by the fact that such visits tend to be made only to the visitor center. The greater values, the experiences of involvement, are passed by.

To a marked extent this same philosophy of interpreting to a visitor rather than involving him in an experience also appears to govern the policies of the United States Fish and Wildlife Service and the United States Forest Service in their effort to provide visitor centers and interpretive programs. In response to a question about his research on some of the botanical aspects of Land Between the Lakes, a professor replied, "The glamor of the unusual should not obscure the significance of the ordinary."[3] The "ordinary" illuminated by appreciation and understanding can inspire visions and establish goals just

[1] Tennessee Valley Authority, *Concept Statement for Land Between the Lakes* (Knoxville, Tenn., April 1964), p. 2.

[2] U. S., Department of the Interior, National Park Service, *First World Conference on National Parks* (Washington, D. C., 1962), p. 13.

[3] Unpublished letter to Robert M. Howes, director of Land Between the Lakes, from Alfred Clebsch, Austin Peay State University, Clarksville, Tenn., Jan. 6, 1967.

as effectively as Old Faithful or Grand Canyon. Likewise, without appreciation and understanding, Old Faithful can be no more than a burst of steam or Grand Canyon no more than a gigantic gully. In Land Between the Lakes there is the constant challenge to raise sights via the "ordinary" to new realms of the human spirit.

That the program focuses in and from the 5,000-acre Conservation Education Center does not imply that it is out of focus elsewhere in the 170,000 acres of Land Between the Lakes. In the Center, however, are concentrated the principal features of greatest interest to the greatest number of visitors. It is the purpose of the Center—as elsewhere throughout Land Between the Lakes—to engage people in the process of learning about conservation so that they in turn can help develop and preserve the nation's resources and its environment. Briefly stated, the aims are fivefold: first, to help people understand the basic facts of resource conservation and development; second, to help define important conservation issues; third, to help people make intelligent choices between competitive uses of the nation's resources; fourth, to help people know and enjoy the out-of-doors; and fifth, above all, to enable people to have a good and satisfying time during their visit.

In the Conservation Education Center will be concentrated a series of stations connected by drives and trails where visitors to Land Between the Lakes will be able to see and to participate in a variety of conservation activities. For example, a series of wildlife stations will enable the visitor to view a beaver lodge and give him places where he may at times see deer, wild geese, turkeys, bald eagles, and other birds and animals. In an arboretum special plantations of desirable plants suggest those that will attract songbirds to his backyard, vacation home, or farm. A series of forestry stations will include demonstrations of how to thin and plant trees or control gullies. In another arboretum native trees will be labeled. A station devoted to fire and grazing damage may also suggest the constructive possibilities of controlled burning and grazing. A series of agricultural stations will acquaint city children with domestic animals and can trace the evolution of some of the hybrid varieties of plants that have helped make the United States a nation of abundance. The best practices in contour farming and the usefulness of a farm pond will be illustrated. A series of historical stations will interpret the region's absorbing history. Although the majority of these stations will be within the Conservation Education Center, some will be elsewhere throughout Land Between the Lakes.

At Center Station visitors from every state in the union are introduced to Land Between the Lakes by means of exhibits that briefly
trace its history and suggest places to see and things to do. Although
these exhibits use the latest audio-visual techniques, their primary aim
is to get the visitor back into the out-of-doors and along trails that
lead him into the forest, across open fields, along the water's edge, or
up to overlooks where he becomes a participant as well as an observer.

At nearby Center Furnace, one of two furnaces remaining from the
dozen or more that once lighted the night skies of the between-the-
rivers area, the visitor can see for himself one of the principal instru-
ments with which man ushered in the age of iron and steel. Interpretive
devices are presently scarce, but will be supplemented.

Nature trails, except one, are mostly surfaced with sod or wood
chips, comfortable underfoot, yet free of hazards that would otherwise
distract the user's attention from wildflowers, trees, ferns, mosses,
lichens, or wildlife denizens and their signs. Where trails cross bogs,
swampy areas, or stream courses, boardwalks and footbridges replace
sod and wood chips. One trail is blacktopped to a width permitting
two wheelchairs to pass. Here those with impaired eyesight, those
confined to wheelchair or crutches, or those having other physical
disabilities may sample a rich section of hardwood forest alongside one
of the few permanent streams in Land Between the Lakes. For each of
these trails, interpretive materials have been prepared or are in preparation.

The Silo Overlook provides visitors to the Conservation Education
Center with vistas across Lake Barkley from near the heart of the area
most favored by migrating flocks of wild geese and other waterfowl.
The silo is the sole physical reminder of the former "Empire Farm"
which flourished during the decade following closure of the iron
industry on the landholdings of the Hillman Land and Iron Company.
Of poured reinforced concrete, the silo once stored corn grown on the
fertile bottomlands that now lie beneath the waters of Lake Barkley.
Its ridge crest location was safely above the spring and winter floods
which frequently covered those cornfields. Now surmounted by an
observation platform reached by a wooden approach ramp, the silo is
enjoying a reincarnation.

The Empire Farm is further perpetuated in the educational farm
of Land Between the Lakes. Here a collection of domestic animals
and crops has been assembled to acquaint (or reacquaint) children of

all ages with what was once commonplace but now known to few city dwellers accustomed only to the supermarket or the corner grocery store as the ultimate source of food. Here the urban child can see, touch, and smell rabbits, poultry, a mare and her colt, a jenny and jack, not to mention a mule. On occasion he may see a cow milked. Perhaps some fall a mule will turn a sorghum mill. Elsewhere about the farm are displays of farm tools, kitchen utensils, and other equipment recalling the days of farming before the age of electricity.

Other educational stations for the general public are still in the planning stage. They include an aquarium; a planetarium; a bird banding station; blinds for the study, painting, and photography of wildlife; and others that experience will dictate. Two stations are intended for more than a brief visit: the Youth Station, already described, and the Adult Station. The latter, to be located in the Conservation Education Center on the shore of Lake Barkley between the Silo Overlook and the Youth Station, is planned as a conference and workshop center for 250 adults. Blueprints call for housing and eating accommodations, classrooms, research laboratories, library, auditorium, and meeting spaces for groups of various sizes up to its full capacity. It will be available for luncheons, workshops, conferences, and colloquiums staged by any group concerned with conservation of the nation's environment and its resources. Universities, high schools, civic clubs, sportsmen's groups, garden clubs, government officials, citizen boards, trade associations, planning commission members, and professional organizations are expected to be among its principal users. Teacher training workshops will find that the nearby Youth Station serves the role of the traditional "campus school" as a life-laboratory for studying and gaining experience with the latest techniques of outdoor education.

TVA expects to supply the facilities and program aids to enable the groups to conduct worthwhile programs for their members. TVA, however, will not provide these programs on its own. Laboratories will be available for both teaching and research. By means of liaison with the university or association of universities, the Adult Station can become a center of national interest for research, teaching, and demonstration in the field of conservation and environmental education and resource development.

Chapter Ten

From Private to Public Ownership

Viewing the physical characteristics of the land between the rivers and the economic uses to which it was being put, it appeared at the outset that the purchase of property for the Land Between the Lakes demonstration would offer fewer difficulties than TVA had experienced in many earlier reservoir acquisitions. The area to be purchased from private owners would amount to some 100,000 acres. Within the area lived 949 families, or one family for each 103 acres on the average. The section was sparsely settled, by any definition.

The incomes of by far the greatest proportion of resident families were modest or low and came mainly from farming. The businesses were country grocery or general stores or gasoline filling stations. There were few restaurants and motels. Eight lakeshore businesses offered various types of fishing and boating services. The three "towns" in the area were hamlets, with the largest approaching only three hundred people.

There were no industries, no railroads. The most extensive public utility service was that provided generally by two rural electric co-operatives. The telephone company had cable extending along the main east-west road and part of the main north-south highway, so the villages and a number of scattered communities had telephone service. There was no public water supply or sewer system. While the main roads were blacktop or otherwise "all weather," the backcountry roads often lacked even a gravel surface and were impassable by automobile in rainy weather. No doctor served the area, and there were no hospitals.

In short, the Land Between the Lakes area had remained as nearly untouched by America's industrializing, urbanizing trends as any area of comparable size in the eastern United States. The task of changing the ownership from a few private hands to all the people of the United States seemed relatively simple.

Yet there were underlying factors, not readily apparent at the outset, which complicated TVA's task of land buying. While the great majority of inhabitants consented—if not willingly, at least cooperatively—to TVA's acquisition, a number of individuals were tenacious in their determination to retain their property. The result was that the Land Between the Lakes land buying program involved some of the most difficult and unique problems in the history of the agency.

TVA's basic policy in approaching the land acquisition task was identical to that of the past which had been regarded as unusually successful. This policy was founded essentially on recognition of the fact that when the government buys land for a public purpose it is normally dealing with an unwilling seller. The owner will be displaced. He will suffer inconvenience and perhaps hardship. Therefore, the purchaser (TVA) should compensate the seller to the extent that he is restored to approximately the same condition of life under which he lived before the move.

The long-standing practice applied to the Land Between the Lakes was to appraise property carefully and fairly and then to make a generous offer which would compensate the owner for his inconvenience, at least in part, as well as the value of his physical holdings. In addition, it had been TVA's practice to provide those who desired it special assistance in locating a new home or farm or area suitable to start up in business again. This practice was also employed in buying Land Between the Lakes.

Other aspects of TVA policy were designed to make the process of moving less onerous personally and financially. For example, an individual whose home or farm was purchased was allowed to live in it, even after TVA had paid for it, until TVA actually needed the property. For some early purchases this elapsed time amounted to more than three years. Or as an alternative, he might relocate to another home and rent his former residence until TVA took it over. A number of Land Between the Lakes residents, in fact, made this latter choice, and the result was the existence of a modest transient population during the period of land purchase. Still another alternative was to allow the owner, at a small reduction in purchase price, to retain his house and other improvements for removal to a new location or for sale to third parties. This choice also was widely exercised by the Land Between the Lakes residents. In addition, farmers whose land was acquired were permitted not only to live on the land but to farm it and retain the income until TVA needed to take possession. The same privilege was extended to operators of stores, filling stations, and other businesses.

Acquiring the land was a three-step process. First, it was surveyed and mapped. Second, it was appraised and an offer made to the owner. And finally, a deed was executed and the money paid. Appraised values were determined after careful study of the market values in the area and several surrounding counties. Courthouse records were studied to find out the kinds of properties which had changed hands and the prices paid in the free market. Experienced appraisers—two, acting independently, in each instance—went over each tract personally, whenever possible in the presence of the owner. All aspects of value were included, and opportunity for discussion was provided.

When an evaluation was determined, however, it was a firm price, not subject to negotiation or trading. Unless it were shown that some element of value had been omitted, the TVA offer would stand unchanged. The reason for this "no-price-trading policy" was TVA's intention to avoid any favoritism or injustice, either in actuality or in appearance, to any landowner. Were the price subject to negotiation, the result would depend as much on the trading ability of the individual as upon the true value of the land, thus favoring those who could afford expert assistance over those who could not.

The property owner could refuse to accept the TVA offer. In such cases, TVA as a government agency could and did exercise the constitutional power of eminent domain, a legal proceeding under which property could be purchased by court order with the compensation being set by the court. The process is commonly referred to as "condemnation." In the entire previous history of TVA land buying, over 96 percent of the tracts purchased had been obtained by acceptance of TVA's offer, less than 4 percent by condemnation. In Land Between the Lakes only 92 percent accepted the TVA offer.

Before land acquisition began, two policy decisions had to be made by the TVA board of directors. Boundaries of the project were established, and the earlier decision to purchase all the land within the boundaries was reaffirmed.

The decision pertaining to boundaries was announced by the TVA board on January 16, 1964. The TVA decided that the natural boundaries on the east and west would be the shorelines, respectively, of Lake Barkley and Kentucky Lake. On the north, the canal joining the two lakes offered a physical barrier making it an advantageous boundary. The southern extremity offered no similar physical or geographic barrier. Near the point where the parallel courses of the Cumberland (Lake Barkley) and the Tennessee (Kentucky Lake) begin to diverge, however, U. S. Highway 79 crossed from one river to the other. This highway was scheduled for upgrading and minor realignment in the near future. It was, therefore, announced that the southern boundary of Land Between the Lakes would be based generally on the relocation route of the new highway from Kentucky Lake east to its crossing of Bear Creek approximately midway between the two bodies of water. From there the boundary would proceed to Lake Barkley in a northerly and easterly direction along the slopes of the ridges lying south of Bear Creek and generally parallel to it. This divergence north from the highway was made in order to exclude the town of Dover and the Fort Donelson military reservation, making use of a natural geographic feature. Establishment of a detailed boundary would have to await accurate surveys of property lines and the details of natural features.

"Private lands left within Land Between the Lakes would be a deterrent to maximum public use of the area," the TVA board said in its announcement, "and to development of commercial facilities across the lakes from this area, and would present serious problems in administration and control of the area." But the most persuasive reason for the total ownership decision lay in the basic concept of Land Between the Lakes development. If those seeking recreation wished to find a place where all signs of the city were absent, then commercial and private establishments—even homes and farms—must also be absent. If new motels and services were to be barred, the older ones must also fall within this bar.

Inevitably, the first property acquired had to be the land most urgently needed to make the area usable by the public for the purposes intended as soon as possible. Fortunately, nearly all the land for these initial purposes was already held by agencies of the federal government.

So that camping and other outdoor public use could begin at an early date, it was decided that the first campground would be located on land already owned by TVA on the eastern shore of Kentucky Lake at the mouth of Rushing Creek in the southern portion of the area.

On the shoreline of the future Lake Barkley to the east, development plans called for expansion and modification of the wildlife program, facilities for large camping groups, and an educational center for teaching conservation and the life sciences in the open. Central to these purposes would be three small impoundments to be created by small earthfill dams across the mouths of Crooked Creek and Long Creek in the northern portion of the area and Bards Creek to the south. These impoundments would provide a constant water level, unaffected by the large periodic fluctuations of the great Barkley reservoir required for flood control, power generation, and commercial navigation. The constant level would also serve best the needs of boating, swimming, and wildlife protection and propagation.

But Barkley Dam was scheduled for completion in the fall of 1965, and the impoundment of its reservoir would make construction of these small dams prohibitively expensive. Work had to begin as soon as possible. Most of the shoreline property was in the custody of the United States Army Corps of Engineers and the Kentucky Woodlands Wildlife Refuge of the United States Fish and Wildlife Service. Agreement in principle had been reached with these agencies on the transfer of their lands to TVA for inclusion in Land Between the Lakes, but construction could not await the time required to complete the legal steps necessary for TVA acquisition.

All three agencies recognized the problem and concluded interim agreements giving TVA the necessary access to all federally owned land for carrying out preliminary work for the program of Land Between the Lakes. This included such essential details as clearing trees and brush, planting half a million pine seedlings already on order in nearby nurseries, and preimpoundment work within the Barkley Reservoir. In April 1964 arrangements were made for TVA to occupy and use the wildlife refuge property for these and other essential purposes.

These arrangements were followed the ensuing January by an interim arrangement giving TVA custodial and administrative responsibility for refuge lands. The Bureau of Sport Fisheries and Wildlife of the United States Fish and Wildlife Service suspended its operations, and employees of the Bureau, at their election, joined TVA's staff or accepted transfers to other areas operated by the Bureau. Subsequently, the Bureau of Sport Fisheries and Wildlife and the Corps of Engineers formally confirmed exchanges of lands and rights in their custody made necessary by the impoundment of Lake Barkley, after which the refuge status of the Kentucky Woodlands area was terminated. The director of the Bureau of the Budget then formally transferred full custody and control of the former refuge lands to TVA.

Some privately owned land was needed for early construction, administration, and other project purposes, but for the most part TVA adopted the policy of acquiring first the land of those individuals who wished to sell quickly, and particularly those for whom delay in moving would involve some special hardship. Requests for early sale were more numerous than TVA could fulfill with the funds available. More than five hundred owners asked TVA to buy their lands as soon as possible.

Every effort was made to establish personal contact with the families of the area to promote understanding of the procedures in the purchase of land and the attention that TVA would give to the problems and inconveniences of having to find and establish a new home. A letter was sent to each property owner, explaining TVA's purchase plans and procedures and telling where further information could be found. Extensive use was made of the nearby news media to convey this type of information, and families were invited to come personally to the TVA offices in Golden Pond. To make such contact easier, temporary offices were set up in motels at the north and south ends of the area. Several hundred took advantage of this invitation.

A family relocation service was established to provide up-to-date information on properties available in the surrounding area—farms, homes, commercial properties, and subdivision lots. In addition, much initiative was undertaken by nearby chambers of commerce, real estate associations, and state and local welfare agencies in extending help to those who requested it. One of the interesting private enterprises that developed during the transition period was the movement of dozens of houses, and even a restaurant, by barge to new locations across Barkley and Kentucky lakes.

Despite the widespread acceptance of the Land Between the Lakes development by most of the people living in the area, many others were skeptical and some remained adamantly opposed. A variety of factors contributed to their attitudes. The concept of an outdoor recreation area as a national asset was new, not only in the region but in the country as a whole; the potential benefits, to the area and to the nation, were therefore not readily apparent to many. Some disputed the TVA decision to take all the land lying between the lakes; they contended that the land already held by federal agencies would be sufficient for the intended purposes. Some property owners had, in fact, been forced to move on one or more previous occasions when one of these agencies had acquired their land; they were determined not to let it happen again. A few undoubtedly saw opportunities for speculative profits. Some public officials were concerned that the removal of land from the tax books would reduce the income of the three counties affected.

Whatever their motives, those unwilling to sell created an organization to make their opposition more effective, calling themselves the Tri-County Organization for Constitutional Rights. It was established soon after the TVA board announced its plans for total acquisition, and its major effort in the succeeding months was an attempt to persuade Congress not to appropriate funds for Land Between the Lakes. A delegation was sent to Washington on several occasions to testify against the development before congressional committees and to call upon individual members of Congress.

Typical of the argumentation used is the following extract from an open letter to the president and Congress inserted in the record of the hearings before the House Appropriations Subcommittee on Public Works:

Many of our people have been bought out and moved four times previously because of Federal projects here. We have clung tenaciously to the land between the rivers and have been squeezed into a small area. Many homes have been moved three times. . . .

The Federal Government owns approximately 100,000 acres of land here which is undeveloped. We are not opposed to the national recreation area so long as land in direct Federal ownership is utilized. Approximately 60,000 acres of timberland in large corporate holdings have been available at a reasonable price for years. In other recreation area developments the villages and communities of natives have been excluded from Federal ownership. They have been left with sizable expansion room to permit their individual growth as tourist centers. We resent the capricious and arbitrary decision TVA has made in our case.

. . . You are talking economy but to buy this land and take it off the county tax rolls is absurd. Half of our counties have already been bought by the Federal Government. We will not have enough taxable property to meet the cost of county government and to retire our bonds predicated on anticipated tax revenue.

Many of our ancestors settled here in the 1700's. We need our homes, businesses, churches and schools much more than we need our land bought up for a haven for opossums, coons, rattlesnakes, and mangy buffalo. There is probably no group of people in the United States who have been repeatedly so tortured at taxpayers' expense, as have we.[1]

The opponents of the project received the important support of Senator Allen J. Ellender of Louisiana, an influential member of the Senate Appropriations Committee and chairman of its Public Works Subcommittee. "The TVA is now trying to enter into a new sphere," Senator Ellender told the Senate during debate on the TVA appropriations in August 1964.

We have provided in the bill approximately $50 million for the purposes of this agency. But the TVA proposes to use part of these funds in embarking on a new program that involves the purchase of land for the purpose of developing a national recreation area. In my opinion the TVA today owns more land than is necessary for it to carry on the projects that it is authorized under the law to carry on. . . .

But what I have objected to, and what I am objecting to now is for the TVA to proceed to buy 100,000 acres and develop that into a park.

It seems to me that if a park is necessary, the project should be turned over to the Park Service. The land purchases and the development should be made by the Park Service instead of the TVA. I have seen no suggestion anywhere that the TVA knows more about park management than does the Park Service, and can "demonstrate" to the Park Service how to run a park. The park is not a demonstration necessary and suitable to any plans TVA is making, but is the end product of plans completed by TVA in 1961.[2]

Testimony in Washington was buttressed by activity in the area. The fiscal courts of Lyon and Trigg counties, Kentucky, voted to oppose the project. So did the Lyon County School Board. A small picket line paraded in front of the TVA offices at Golden Pond from time to time. A sit-in at the office of the Recorder of Deeds in Lyon County

[1] U. S., Congress, House of Representatives, Subcommittee on Public Works Appropriations, *Public Works Appropriations for 1965, Hearings before a Subcommittee of the Committee on Appropriations*, 88th Cong., 2d sess., 1964, pt. 4: 870-71.

[2] U. S., Congress, Senate, *Congressional Record*, 88th Cong., 2d sess., Aug. 7, 1964, p. 18514.

hampered for a time TVA's examination of property transfer records.

Unfounded rumors and events heightened the problem. An outdoor writer wrote that the wild turkey flock in the Kentucky Woodlands Wildlife Refuge would be transferred to Tennessee. An official "learned" that TVA was buying land purportedly for recreation while intending to sell it for industrial use. A rifle bullet was fired through the door of the TVA land office one night. A house about to be moved to a barge for transport across Kentucky Lake was destroyed by a fire of unknown origin.

TVA continued its active efforts during this period to explain the project to the people, make its procedures clear, and put down unfounded rumors and charges. Announcements were made to the press, and TVA administrators responded frequently to requests from local groups to speak about the project.

The hearings in Congress reflected widespread support as well as opposition. Stewart County, Tennessee, one of three counties affected, endorsed the plan. The two state governors gave it their backing, and the Kentucky state legislature adopted a favorable resolution. The committees received numerous letters and telegrams from mayors and county officials, civic clubs, labor unions, and citizens backing the project. The principal newspaper in the immediate area, the *Paducah Sun-Democrat,* gave it knowledgeable support. The appropriation as recommended by the president was approved.

Although this initial effort to stop Land Between the Lakes failed, the activities of those in opposition did not end. They contended, despite clear facts to the contrary, that the development had adversely affected the revenues of county government. A legal battle challenged the constitutional and statutory right of TVA to buy land for the purposes of Land Between the Lakes. They attempted to show that the people of the isthmus area had suffered physically, mentally, and financially.

The county tax problem had a number of complex aspects. The short story is that the three counties derived a total of about $45,000 of tax revenue from the land prior to its purchase by TVA. By the middle of 1968 they were receiving from TVA, in lieu of taxes, over $95,000, more than double their previous tax revenue. TVA had anticipated the tax problem of the counties early in the project planning. It had worked out the steps required for a solution and early in 1964 discussed them with officials of the states of Tennessee and Kentucky. The states agreed with TVA's proposals and put them into effect. In addition, TVA worked out an agreement with the United States Department of Health, Education, and Welfare which maintained, and even slightly increased for the Land Between the Lakes counties, the payments which the federal government makes to local school systems when they are affected by programs and activities of the United States government.

The legal fight over TVA land acquisition was carried to the United States District Court for the Western District of Kentucky in a challenge to a suit brought by TVA to acquire certain property by condemnation when the owners declined to accept TVA's offer. The owners charged, among other things, that TVA had "no legal authority, reason or necessity" to buy or condemn the land; that it was "acting arbitrarily, capriciously and in bad faith"; that the amount of land being purchased was "in excess of the requirements"; and that the acquisition and use of the land was "violative of the Constitution and laws of the United States."

In an opinion handed down October 17, 1968, Judge Henry L. Brooks held, "There is no merit to any of these multifarious objections." He held that the TVA Act of 1933 as amended contained sufficient legal authority for TVA to undertake the Land Between the Lakes development and buy the land necessary for that purpose. "The taking of this land for the Land Between the Lakes demonstration," he wrote, "is not contrary to the Constitution and laws of the United States. The statutory laws of the United States . . . authorize the taking, and the project for which the land is taken is to demonstrate how the proper use, conservation and development of natural resources can stimulate the physical, economical and social development of the area. Such a project is authorized under the commerce clause and the general welfare clause of the Constitution."[3]

A similar suit brought in United States District Court for the Middle District of Tennessee, concerning land in Stewart County, Tennessee, resulted in a similar judgment by Judge William E. Miller.

During the summer of 1968 an attempt was made to obtain national backing for the effort to block the development of Land Between the Lakes. It was conducted in collaboration with a representative of the American Landowners Association with headquarters in Harpers Ferry,

[3] *United States ex rel. TVA* v. *Davis,* Civil No. 1747 (W. D. Ky., Oct. 17, 1968).

West Virginia. Statements were obtained from some sixty-odd individuals alleging various forms of TVA injustice and harassment. TVA thoroughly investigated all the charges. Some of the signers refused to talk to the TVA representatives, and others gave information in direct conflict with other reports given to TVA. A number of complaints obviously were the result of misunderstandings. And by far the greatest number rested on the contention that they were not being paid enough for their land.

Although they were frankly reluctant to face the prospect of a move from a familiar environment, the overwhelming majority of individuals and families in the Land Between the Lakes made changes which they later agreed resulted in a better mode of living. They moved from the isolation of a remote rural area where the services and conveniences which most people take for granted were rare. They took up life anew for the most part in the midst of small communities where electricity and water and sanitation facilities were available, where the roads were blacktopped, and where a doctor or hospital was nearby.

Mrs. Mary Baker, a schoolteacher with a master's degree and widow of a farmer, tearfully disposed of her frame house and the land where she and her husband had spent their married life. She reinvested in property which gave her a rental income, and she now lives in a modern brick home thirty miles closer to her school.

Bill Futrell was a young farmer earning a satisfactory living on his land, but his three children had to go fifteen miles to school over roads that were subject to washouts that left them isolated for days at a time. Their boarded log home could have been modernized only at great expense. Their new home is much closer to schools, grocery stores, doctors, and farm markets. His farming abilities can now be used more productively.

A couple in their fifties—Mr. and Mrs. Maxie Barrett—the husband an invalid, lived on welfare in a house without bath or electricity, dependent on neighbors for shopping and transportation. They moved to a community where their needs could be satisfied close at hand.

Mr. and Mrs. Flaveous Boren were an elderly couple living in a shack lined with cardboard and heated with a wood fire. They carried water from a spring a mile away. Their move brought them electric heat, running water with bath and a washing machine, and bus service a block away.

An entire community of twenty families sold their properties, which included a deteriorating motel, and relocated across the lake a few miles away, with a modern motel and improved homes and businesses.

The few businesses in the 170,000-acre area were among the first to request TVA to purchase their properties. At final count, these consisted of twenty general mercantile stores of which seventeen had gasoline pumps, eight service stations, six motels, eight resorts of various types, nine restaurants, and three bait-and-tackle shops. The grocery-store type of businesses were anxious to move before TVA bought out too many of their customers. Realizing that it takes time to reestablish a clientele, they wanted to relocate as soon as possible.

Two rural electric cooperatives—the Pennyrile Rural Electric Cooperative Corporation and the Cumberland Electric Membership Corporation—provided electric service to the residents of the properties between the lakes. They remained in business in the area providing electricity to the new TVA development. The main problem was a matter of adjustment during the interim. It was anticipated that as land was purchased and residents moved, demands for electricity would decline. They would be offset to some extent, however, by the growing requirements of the Land Between the Lakes installations themselves.

Most of the nearly 1,860 ownerships in Land Between the Lakes were relatively small, ranging in size from a single building lot to farms that seldom exceeded 1,000 acres. Two large holdings, however, involved almost one-third of all the private land acquired for the program and required no displacement of people. The acquisition of each of these holdings set new records in the entire history of TVA land acquisition. Largest was the Koppers property totaling 15,151 acres. This holding had been managed for several years according to a sound commercial timber management plan but consisted largely of interior tracts without frontage on highways or lakeshore. The Wells Heath family holdings of some 14,200 acres likewise consisted of scattered interior tracts assembled by a single individual over a period of years as farms were abandoned or sold for taxes or estates were settled.

The acquisition of church and cemetery properties presented a number of unusual situations. There were twenty-nine church structures in the area and some two hundred cemeteries, some with burials going back to the early 1800s and perhaps earlier. A number of the structures had been virtually abandoned by their congregations and others were seldom used, perhaps once or twice a year for memorial services and decoration of graves. But several had active congregations, and both the structures and the institutions were matters of great spiritual and sentimental value to their members. TVA undertook to make its policies as flexible in meeting the wishes of these congregations and of the families or trustees of the cemeteries as was feasible and consistent with the objectives of the total program.

The churches, most of them small and of frame construction, were, of course, landmarks of the area and social and religious centers of the communities in which they were located. If not used and cared for regularly by their congregations, however, they would face a hazardous existence from potential fire and vandalism. TVA, therefore, sought out the parties responsible for the physical properties of each congregation. Ultimately, purchase agreements were reached with trustees or other authorized representatives of every church organization owning land or other properties in the area. Under these agreements, a dozen or more congregations took the funds from the TVA purchase to build new churches on sites outside Land Between the Lakes. Others merged with congregations outside the area and combined their funds to improve or build new structures on the outside. Still others, finding their memberships already widely dispersed, decided to disband and distribute the purchase funds to charitable causes. The Model Baptist Church, for example, gave $2,000 and their pastor's home and contents to its minister; gave $12,000 to the building funds of three other Baptist churches; and allocated the income from the remainder equally among denominational children's homes, foreign missions, and home missions. The Golden Pond Baptist Church distributed $7,000 to three Kentucky homes for children. The Roman Catholic diocese used its funds to build a church serving a newly formed congregation in Cadiz. Still other churches established funds for perpetual care of their cemeteries.

TVA acquired one church, the Azotus Christian Church, on Lick Creek in Stewart County, Tennessee, for the purpose of moving it to a central location for preservation as a symbol of the numerous rural churches that once served the people between the rivers. Here visitors will be able to see an example of the physical surroundings in which the people of the area once worshiped. From time to time appropriate services and meetings will be held within the structure or on its surrounding grounds.

TVA also provided means by which congregations and other interested people could preserve and use rural church structures. This could be done by creating a nonprofit corporation which would enter into a contract with TVA to maintain the property as a historic shrine. The corporation would assume responsibility for the structure and for the safety of the public using it. By arrangement with the corporation the structure would remain available for funerals, memorial services, homecomings, and similar activities consistent with the original purpose. People interested in preserving the Woodson Chapel Church overlooking Lake Barkley from the former community of Mont, for example, elected to follow this alternative.

In the case of cemeteries, TVA determined at an early date that these, with their more than 9,000 graves, could remain in place without interfering with the essential activities of Land Between the Lakes. It was thought that these cemeteries in future years would become of growing interest to millions of visitors. Man reveres the burial places of his dead, and reverence has a place in leisure time pursuits for even the most single-minded recreation seekers. Accordingly, the terms of acquisition provided that the cemeteries in Land Between the Lakes will remain accessible for visiting, decoration, and normal maintenance. Additional burials are permitted as long as space is available. If conflicting uses occur in the vicinity of the cemeteries, TVA will accept responsibility for protective measures, such as fencing. An exhaustive program of locating and mapping all cemeteries and assembling all existing records was undertaken. Where possible, the occupant of each grave was identified. Painstakingly accurate, the records thus assembled are, in most if not all cases, the only ones available. When future burials occur, they will be recorded. Copies of the records are kept on file at the Golden Pond headquarters where they may be consulted by any interested person.

Each of these policies and actions was shaped by TVA to recognize, in acquiring the properties within Land Between the Lakes, the human needs, desires, and aspirations of the people who lived there and to preserve the sites and symbols of their history and culture. Homes and businesses are gone, but the people who return or the visitors who come for the first time can still see the physical evidence of a way of life which tried hard, struggled manfully, but never quite succeeded.

The names that emerged from this struggle—the names that the people gave to their roads and landmarks—are still in use. The community of Energy gave its name to Camp Energy, a campground for Boy Scouts, Girl Scouts, and other organizations. Silver Trail still leads to Center Furnace, but from the opposite direction. Today it rewards the visitor with frequent glimpses of wildlife and history as it once rewarded ironworkers who regularly lined its route to await the visit of the paymaster. Shaw Branch still drains Boardinghouse Hollow although its mouth in Crooked Creek lies submerged beneath the waters of Lake Barkley. Lake access areas, used almost daily by campers, fishermen, and boaters, perpetuate the names of the Nickell and Neville families, settlers of the area in the eighteenth century. Ferry landings which once provided the only access to the area are perpetuated by such names as Hillman, Birmingham, Eddyville, and Boswell.

In all, Land Between the Lakes today comprises 170,000 acres. Of this, TVA itself originally owned 4,000 acres along the shore of Kentucky Lake. The Kentucky Woodlands Wildlife Refuge covered 59,000 acres, and the Corps of Engineers had acquired 12,000 acres for the Barkley Dam and reservoir. The remainder, 95,000 acres, was purchased from private owners. It was made up of 2,427 separate tracts having 1,860 separate ownerships, which were acquired at a total cost of approximately $28,000,000, including acquisition expense. The purchases involved 949 resident families embracing 2,738 people, as well as numerous nonresidents who had left the area and others who had planned to use their properties for retirement.

On July 1, 1969, all land purchases had been completed or were referred to the courts for condemnation proceedings. Of the acreage which had to be acquired from private owners, 85,549 acres were acquired without a contest as to price. The remainder, 10,327 acres, was acquired by condemnation for refusal to sell.

Chapter Eleven

The Natural Environment

LAND BETWEEN THE LAKES has a great abundance and variety of plant and animal life. Without this plant and animal life that is so often taken for granted, TVA's goal of serving the recreational and conservation education needs of millions of Americans could never be realized. In the last century much of the hardwood forest between the rivers was exploited for timber and charcoal production, and by the turn of the twentieth century many of the wildlife species in the area had been wiped out or reduced to dangerously low levels. The graceful white-tailed deer was completely exterminated, and the wild turkey had all but vanished from the area. With the decline of the iron industry between the rivers in the early 1900s the demand for charcoal diminished, and the once great hardwood forest began a slow healing process. Many parts of the area would never regain their glory.

The keen foresight and concerted efforts of two local landowners probably saved the wild turkey from extinction; and in 1919 a large tract of land in the Kentucky portion of the area owned by the Hillman Land Company, Inc., was declared a state game refuge, and deer were restocked. Wildlife populations fluctuated in the ensuing years with the degree of protection provided. The real breakthrough for wildlife came in 1938 when approximately 40,000 acres, including former lands of the Hillman Land Company, were designated a national wildlife refuge by presidential proclamation. This was later expanded to nearly 60,000 acres, and wildlife populations gradually increased under the management and protection of the refuge. The goals of TVA are to maintain the wide variety of plant and animal life in the area and, through proper management and creation of new habitat, increase their numbers where desirable for the fullest enjoyment of all who visit Land Between the Lakes.

FLORA

The plant life in Land Between the Lakes is rich and varied in comparison to that of many areas of similar size in the United States. Over 80 percent of the isthmus is blanketed with a hardwood forest, and the open fields and gently sloping valleys are covered with a wide and colorful variety of herbaceous plants. More than eight hundred species of flowering plants have been identified, and others will undoubtedly be found in the future. Many of these plants have brightly colored flowers, and many others have leaves that display a rainbow of color in the fall.

One of the most interesting times to visit Land Between the Lakes is during the spring when the first flowers begin to appear. Among the earliest of these is the spring beauty, a small plant found scattered over the forest floor. The most spectacular sights, however, are the floral displays of serviceberry, wild plum, redbud, dogwood, and black locust that follow in sequence beginning in late March or early April and continuing through mid-May.

Although oaks and hickories are the predominant woody species, sweet gum, maple, poplar, dogwood, redbud, and many other deciduous species are found in abundance throughout Land Between the Lakes. Conifers (red cedar and pine) make up only a small percentage of the forest acreage.

Most of the plants that grow in the forests and open fields of Land Between the Lakes are native to the area, but some such as dandelion and honeysuckle are exotic or domestic species that have escaped from yards and gardens. Forsythia, peach, japonica, jonquils, and other cultivated plants are also seen around old home sites. Many of the domestic species found in the open lands have been planted for wildlife food and cover, agricultural uses, or erosion control.

The combination of hardwood forests and spacious, open fields that stretches from shoreline to shoreline throughout much of Land Between the Lakes provides an ideal habitat for deer, turkey, songbirds, and other wildlife. And there are miles of trails and backwoods roads that wind their way through the green canopied forest, providing visitors an ideal opportunity to study wildlife, wildflowers, and other plant life in a natural setting. By helping to maintain and improve this delicate balance between wildlife and plant life, the staff of Land Between the Lakes hopes to make the area more enjoyable for all visitors, be they campers, boaters, fishermen, hunters, birdwatchers, or classroom students.

Trees and herbaceous plants are the most familiar plants to the majority of visitors, but there is a whole world of other plant life, each species unique and important. Among these plant groups are the ferns, mosses, liverworts, lichens, algae, and fungi. Most of these plants, with the exception of the algae, which are largely aquatic, are terrestial and grow in the forest under the cover of the larger trees and shrubs.

One of the most interesting of the twenty ferns that have been found in the area is the resurrection fern, so named because of its amazing ability to go from a wilted, dried condition to a turgid, upright state within a few minutes after it is watered. Many of the fern species are quite common and can be seen throughout much of the forested area and along trails and backcountry drives.

One hundred and fifteen species of mosses and twenty species of liverworts have been identified in Land Between the Lakes. Mosses are usually bright green in color and are commonly found growing in patches on the soil or on the bark of trees. Although easily identified as a group, individual species of mosses are difficult to identify, even for an experienced naturalist. The liverworts, so named because many species have lobes similar to a liver, are close relatives of the mosses and are also found growing on trees and moist soil near a swamp or stream.

One of the most common plant groups, and perhaps the least known and understood, is the lichens. The lichens are unique because they are actually two plants in one, an alga and a fungus living together for mutual benefit. They come in a variety of colors, but most appear as green or grayish-green blots on tree bark, rocks, or other surfaces. Eighty-one species of lichens have been identified in Land Between the Lakes, and several others are believed to occur.

Without algae, the tiny, single-celled or filamentous plants that inhabit the lakes, streams, and ponds in and around Land Between the Lakes, the excellent crappie and bass fishing that anglers now enjoy would cease to exist. Although algal growth is sometimes called "scum" or "moss," it is these tiny plants that are responsible for producing much of the oxygen and food necessary to support fish and other aquatic creatures.

Many species of fungi, some spectacular and some very insignificant, grow in Land Between the Lakes. Most visitors are familiar with the large members of the group—the mushrooms, toadstools, shelf-fungi, and puffballs—but few realize that many of the small spots and blemishes on bark, leaves, and fruits are caused by fungi or that fungi are one of the main groups of organisms responsible for decay and disintegration of fallen trees and other plant debris.

In an area such as Land Between the Lakes where major emphasis is placed on conservation education and outdoor recreation, it is imperative that the plant life be identified and classified so that visitors might be able to recognize and to relate names to species seen along roads and trails. The availability of this information will also encourage people to study the natural history of plant groups and individual species. One of the primary benefits is the encouragement of research in the area by scientists, students, and other outside groups interested in nature study.

In 1965 TVA contracted for Austin Peay State University, Clarksville, Tennessee, to conduct inventories of some of the plant and animal groups in Land Between the Lakes. The plant groups studied were flowers, trees and shrubs, ferns, mosses and liverworts, and lichens. The purposes of the studies were to determine the number of species in each group and to gather information on the distribution of each species. These studies were begun in the spring of 1965 by scientists in the Biology Department of the school and continued through the summer of 1967. In any study of this type it is nearly impossible to find all the species inhabiting an area, and it is anticipated that others will be added to the list from time to time. This should be an incentive for amateur naturalists, students, and other visitors to try to find additional species.

During the studies, collections were made of each species and placed in the Austin Peay State University herbarium collection. Colored slides were also made and are available for reference. Many of these slides will be used in booklets that will be published for use as field guides by visitors to the area. As a result of the Austin Peay studies, the following color booklets on plant life are planned for publication: "Spring Flowers of Land Between the Lakes," "Summer and Fall Flowers of Land Between the Lakes," "Trees and Shrubs of Land Between the Lakes," "Ferns of Land Between the Lakes," and "Foliose and Fructicose Lichens of Land Between the Lakes." Studies on other plant and animal groups and subsequent publication of additional illustrated booklets are planned.

FAUNA

Wildlife would undoubtedly head the list of the greatest year-round attractions in Land Between the Lakes. The abundant animal life provides a wide variety of recreational and educational opportunities for many Americans responding to the natural urge to seek new and exciting experiences in the out-of-doors.

Most campers, fishermen, hunters, and nature lovers are familiar with many of the mammals, birds, and fishes that inhabit the area surrounding them. Other less familiar animal life such as the amphibians, reptiles, crustaceans, insects, and lower forms far exceed the familiar groups in number of species and are equally important in nature's scheme.

The life histories of most animals, including man, are complex and many factors influence their life cycle. The tiny water flea which inhabits the waters of Land Between the Lakes feeds upon algae and bacteria and, in turn, may be eaten by a minnow, and the minnow devoured by a larger fish. Completing the cycle, the fish may be eaten by a larger fish, or scooped up by a bald eagle or an osprey, or land in a fisherman's creel, or it may die and provide nourishment for insects, fish, or other small animals, and eventually for plants. Each animal, no matter how small or insignificant, contributes to the benefit of all those who enjoy living, playing, and studying in the out-of-doors. It is important to be aware that delicate balances exist between animal and plant life in order to help conserve and protect them.

Birds are among the most interesting and often observed forms of wildlife in Land Between the Lakes. The area is fortunate in being located on one of the major migration routes, the Mississippi Flyway, where many species of migrant birds pass through each year. Many of the 224 species of birds that have been identified in Land Between the Lakes are songbirds, although a rich variety of waterfowl and shorebirds may be seen along lake shorelines. Birdwatchers frequent the area several times each year to conduct bird counts and to study and enjoy nature. Birds are among the most rewarding groups of wildlife to study, primarily because they are colorful, ubiquitous, and will frequently allow observers to study them at close range.

Some species of birds are seen in Land Between the Lakes year-round. Among these are the bobwhite quail and the wild turkey, one of the most magnificent game birds in America. The wild turkey in Land

Between the Lakes, which may weigh twenty pounds or more, is an original, pure strain. Although similar in appearance to the common domestic turkey, the wild turkey is slimmer and the tail band is buff instead of white. A mature gobbler, in contrast to the hen, is larger, darker in color, and has a beard located on the lower neck. During the mating season the gobbler commonly struts, a term used to describe an exhibition in which the wings are lowered, body feathers are fluffed, and tail feathers are spread as the bird gobbles and slowly walks along.

The wild turkey survives best in areas of mature forest with numerous small clearings. Especially desirable is the situation where there is an oak-hickory forest composed of large trees with relatively open areas under the tree canopy. Turkeys nest on the ground but roost high in trees. The average nest contains eleven eggs which are pale buff, evenly spotted with purplish-gray, and hatch in about twenty-eight days. Visitors should avoid disturbing a nest, since the hen may subsequently desert it. Turkeys are strong flyers for short distances, but usually walk over most of the large area comprising their home range. Their diet is composed primarily of seeds and fruits, but they may eat various insects and other small invertebrates. Turkeys are extremely wary creatures and are, therefore, rarely seen by visitors, except perhaps for a fleeting glance along roadways. The best chance to see one of these majestic birds is to hike to a remote, open valley in early morning during the spring and summer. In the fall and winter the birds obtain most of their food from the forest and do not often frequent openings. During the mating season in April and early May the males are frequently heard gobbling from just before sunrise until two or three hours after daylight.

The birds of prey are among the most fascinating and mysterious groups of birds in Land Between the Lakes. Six species of owls have been recorded, but the most common is the barred owl. Many fishermen and campers are familiar with the haunting hoot heard in the quiet, lowland forest areas and along the lakeshore. The barred owls may be heard throughout the year, but they are most vocal during mid-winter when mating and nesting begin. Owls, the earliest nesting birds in Land Between the Lakes, usually nest in January and February.

Another common bird of prey is the red-tailed hawk. This big bird with light underside is frequently seen soaring high above the treetops, scanning the terrain below for mice and other small mammals which make up a large portion of his diet. The red-tailed hawk is also seen perched in trees along roadways or utility line rights-of-way. Like most other hawks and falcons in the area, he is extremely wary, but has become somewhat adjusted to motor vehicles passing nearby.

Among the most regal birds that visit Land Between the Lakes are the bald eagle and golden eagle. From November to April, these birds visit the area from their northern nesting grounds. The bald eagle, although by far the rarest of the two throughout the country, is much more common here than the golden eagle. Nevertheless, only about fifty of these birds are estimated to be in Land Between the Lakes during the peak population in mid-February. The golden eagle population in the area is probably never greater than ten. Eagles have wingspreads of up to seven and one-half feet and would be quite easily spotted and identified if it were not for the fact that they are usually seen at great distances, thereby making it difficult to distinguish them. An adult bald eagle with its dark body and its white head and tail is usually quite easily distinguished, particularly when binoculars are used, but an immature bird may easily be confused with a golden eagle or the vultures and large hawks. The best place to observe bald eagles is along the wooded shoreline of the quiet bays and coves of Kentucky Lake and Lake Barkley. Duncan Bay on Kentucky Lake and Fulton Bay on Lake Barkley are favorite eagle haunts, although any of the large bays may harbor one or more bald eagles. It is not uncommon to find more than one bird perched in the same tree or to see several soaring at the same time. The ideal time to look for them is during mid-February in the early daylight hours when they are most likely to be soaring.

Autumn marks the return of migratory water birds to Land Between the Lakes and their southern wintering grounds. Various species of shorebirds may be seen at this time along the mudflats or flying low over the water. Gulls and terns are seen in great numbers at times, the gulls sometimes forming small "islands" as they flock close together on shallow flats in the large lakes. Most of these shorebirds move on further south for the winter after pausing at Land Between the Lakes. A few, such as the green heron, occasionally nest in the area during the summer.

One of the most thrilling sounds in outdoor life is the distant honking of the great Canada geese as they wing their way southward during the first crisp days of fall. Each year during migration several thousand Canada geese and a variety of ducks stop at Land Between the Lakes to feed on the tender grasses and grains provided for them. Each species has its own particular time of peak migration. Some of the handsome birds feed for a few days and then proceed on south, but thousands of others spend the winter in the area.

A favorite spot to observe part of the wintering flock of geese is the Silo Overlook, along the Lake Barkley shoreline in the Conservation Education Center. Both geese and ducks spend much of the day and the night in protected bays along the lakeshore, but during the early daylight hours and just before dark they become active and begin flying to and from the feeding grounds. It is at this time that they can be seen winging low over the horizon.

Flocks of feeding ducks are interesting to watch. Their action is characterized by splashing of water and a variety of guttural noises, including the occasional, sudden, loud quacking of a hen mallard. The routine of feeding and resting lasts for many days and weeks until the days get longer and the first hints of spring appear. It is then that the birds begin their long trip northward to the nesting grounds. The wood duck is the only migratory wild duck that commonly nests in the area. They usually nest in hollow trees near the water, but occasionally they use artificial nest boxes provided for them.

A few of the Canada geese and mallard ducks do not migrate but remain in Land Between the Lakes year-round. Most of these birds are part of nonmigratory home flocks of semiwild birds that have been established. Nesting islands have been provided in Honker Lake, a subimpoundment of Lake Barkley. These home flocks provide waterfowl for summer visitors to enjoy and photograph, and they also serve to attract and entice passing wild geese and ducks to stop in the area.

There are approximately thirty species of wild mammals in Land Between the Lakes. They range in size from the least shrew, a predator about the size of your thumb, to the white-tailed deer. The habits of many of the mammals make them difficult to observe. Most are nocturnal or move about primarily during the early daylight hours or just before dark. Visitors interested in seeing or studying wildlife in Land Between the Lakes are recommended to walk the trails or drive slowly over the many backcountry roads during the early morning or late afternoon hours. Another wildlife observation technique is to seek quietly the nearest cover adjacent to one of the woods openings or large, open fields and remain as motionless as possible while waiting for wildlife to appear.

The gray squirrel, a common sight even to most city dwellers, is quite abundant in Land Between the Lakes, particularly where large oak trees abound. Its larger cousin, the fox squirrel, distinguished by its red pelage (coat), is less abundant but may be seen occasionally in small, cutover timber near the forest edge. Fox squirrels are also seen along roadsides and fencerows.

The flying squirrel, a much smaller mammal with a skin fold extending from the sides of the body out the legs to the feet, has been identified in the area, but is rarely seen due to its nocturnal nature. Flying squirrels do not fly, but sail through the air by extending their legs at right angles to their bodies, forming a large air surface with the skin fold. They can regulate their flight by tilting to allow air to escape from one side or the other and by using the tail as a steering device. After climbing high in a tree, they can glide for long distances to the ground, to other trees, or to any point of lower elevation.

Both the red fox and the gray fox are common in Land Between the Lakes and are seen occasionally along roadways and the edges of open fields. A fox travels several miles each night in search of meadow mice, white-footed mice, or other prey. Red foxes seem to enjoy being chased by dogs and will usually avoid running into a den or other inaccessible place unless the dogs get too close. Gray foxes will take shelter when chased by dogs, and unlike red foxes, can easily climb a tree.

Beaver, muskrats, mink, and raccoons are nocturnal animals that may be seen near water throughout most of Land Between the Lakes. The raccoon is the most common of this group and occasionally may be seen near campsites and picnic areas. The beaver is rarely seen, but its sign is abundant around the shorelines of the area, particularly around Hematite Lake in the Conservation Education Center. He is a large rodent, normally weighing from twenty-five to sixty-five pounds and has a reddish-brown coat. Beavers have many anatomical adaptations for their role in nature. The front teeth are large and chisellike for gnawing down trees; the lips are close behind the two front teeth to allow the animal to gnaw under water. The large, webbed, hind feet make the beaver a powerful swimmer. The claws on the hind feet are specialized for combing the body fur. The tail is used for support while gnawing and eating, as a steering device while swimming, and to slap the water as a warning signal to other beaver. Musk (castor) and oil glands are characteristic of the species.

The beaver, like man, can modify his own environment to make it more suitable. Trees and shrubs that are gnawed down furnish, twigs, buds, and bark for food and structural material for lodges and dams. Most of the beaver in Land Between the Lakes live in lakes and do not build dams, since the water is already of sufficient depth for them to float trees and brush to the desired locations. Some beaver live in lodges composed of brush, mud, and grass, while others live in bank dens. Their food consists mostly of tender shoots, twigs, and bark, although they may eat grasses, sedges, and other plants, especially in spring and summer. They are highly adaptable animals and can stay under water for as long as fifteen minutes.

One of the rarest and most beautiful of all mammals in Land Between the Lakes is the bobcat or wildcat, as he is sometimes called. They are long-legged and large in appearance, but usually weigh between fifteen and thirty-five pounds. Contrary to popular opinion, bobcats are extremely shy and unaggressive and make every effort to stay away from people. Their preferred habitat is heavy forest cover with thick underbrush, rock outcroppings, and small clearings. They use thickets, hollow logs, trees, small caves, and dens as resting places during the day. Their foods consist mostly of small animals, including mice, shrews, rats, cottontail rabbits, squirrels, opossums, and various birds. The most common indications of their presence are tracks in mud or snow. Bobcats are night hunters and are rarely seen except when crossing roads.

Two other mammals that are familiar to most people are the opossum and the skunk. Each has its own technique for escaping danger, but is reluctant to use it unless absolutely necessary. If attacked, a skunk will turn its posterior toward the offender, raise its tail, and squirt a vile-smelling musk up to ten feet. This will usually stop even the most formidable enemy, and the skunk goes on about its business of looking for insects and other food. One of the greatest enemies of the skunk is the great horned owl which attacks silently from above.

The opossum has the ability to feign death or "play 'possum" when attacked. Some investigators believe the animal actually goes into a state of shock or faint. In any event, the opossum has survived through the ages when many other animals have not. It is the most primitive mammal in North America and is closely related to the kangaroo and other pouched mammals of Australia. It is the only North American mammal that can hang upside down by its tail; it may also use its tail to carry leaves, sticks, and other materials. Opossums are only about one-half inch long at birth and weigh less than 1/150 ounce. The young leave the pouch at about two and one-half months and may follow the mother or ride on her back or tail.

Two species of deer inhabit Land Between the Lakes, the white-tailed and the fallow. The white-tailed deer, a thin, long-legged mammal, is one of the most proud and graceful of all animals. The females (does) usually weigh from 75 to 150 pounds, while the males (bucks) weigh from 125 to 250 pounds. Bucks are antlered after their first year, but females and fawn bucks normally lack antlers. Antlers are lost during midwinter, but a new set is grown in the spring. The young (fawns) have spots until they are about five months old. Adults are a reddish-brown during the summer and a grayish-brown during the winter. The large tail, which is white on the underside, is displayed when the animal is alarmed, and this is often the fleeting gimpse that many visitors get along the roadsides and trails in Land Between the Lakes. White-tailed deer prefer brushy and forest-bordered fields, but they may occasionally be seen in open fields or in dense forests. During the spring in early morning and late afternoon, they are commonly seen feeding on tender grasses and clovers along the roadsides and in open fields. Much of the diet during other seasons consists of twigs, leaves, and acorns.

The fallow deer, an exotic species, was introduced into Land Between the Lakes around 1920 and has since increased to fairly large numbers in the northern half of the area. They are stockier than the white-tailed deer, but shorter legged and lighter in weight. The color of individuals varies from nearly white to almost black, but most are grayish-brown with a few spots on the sides and hips. There is a black line down the back extending over the upper surface of the tail. Older bucks have large, heavy antlers that are flattened at the tip, similar to those of the moose. Fallow deer feed more on grasses and clovers than do white-tailed deer and consequently are seen more frequently in open fields. It is not uncommon to see these deer in herds of up to twenty animals. During the fall, winter, and spring fallow deer are often seen along roadsides and in green fields in the early morning and late afternoon. The fallow buck is considered a prize trophy among most hunters.

With the exception of the gray squirrel, the mammal that visitors are most likely to see is the woodchuck (groundhog). Chucks are grayish-brown with a reddish cast and appear larger than their six to twelve pounds. He is a stocky rodent with powerful short legs, small ears, and a flattened tail of medium length composed of dark, coarse hairs. Woodchucks usually dig their dens near a forest border, fencerow, or a rock pile, but some are located in open meadows. They feed chiefly on succulent grasses and clovers. They rarely get over fifty yards from their den and intermittently stop to sit and sniff the air and look about. If danger is present, they will scamper back to their dens, usually stop at the entrance for a final look, and then go below. If everything is quiet, they will normally appear at the den entrance within ten minutes. They can usually be seen in early morning and late afternoon during the spring, summer, and fall, but they sleep through most of the winter.

In years past other species of large mammals such as the timber wolf, black bear, elk, and bison (buffalo) ranged throughout Land Between the Lakes, but these animals disappeared before the turn of this century. There are no present plans to restock any of these animals in a wild state in Land Between the Lakes, but a small herd of buffalo now lives in a large meadow in the southern portion of the area. The buffalo provide a link with the past and an opportunity for visitors to enjoy some of the sights that greeted the first settlers to this country.

The herptiles (reptiles and amphibians) are an extremely interesting group of animals to those who ignore the prejudices, fears, and untruths that have been perpetuated against them through the centuries. One of the popular misconceptions is the idea that reptiles are aggressive toward humans. Nothing could be further from the truth. It is true that in many instances snakes may make no effort to avoid human beings, but verified reports of actual aggressiveness are practically unheard of on this continent. Perhaps no other group of animals has been so persecuted with so little justification.

Forty-one species of reptiles and twenty-eight species of amphibians have been recorded in Land Between the Lakes. Turtles, lizards, and snakes make up the reptile group. Most of these species are quite harmless to human beings, although four species of poisonous snakes occur in the area. These are the copperhead, the timber rattler, the pigmy rattler, and the cottonmouth. The poisonous species are rarely encountered. During the warm months turtles can be seen in large numbers basking in the sun on logs and mudbanks along the shores of the lakes and ponds. A lizard is occasionally seen to scamper up a tree or along a fallen log along a trail or path. A colorful variety of toads, frogs, and salamanders represents the amphibians. One of the most common of the frogs, the bullfrog, is recognized by most campers.

Fish probably receive more human attention than any other form of wildlife in Land Between the Lakes. Yet few visitors can accurately identify more than a half dozen of the estimated seventy-five species of fish found in waters in and around the area. Those that are best known are the largemouth bass, crappie, white bass, bluegill, channel catfish, and carp. Many species of fish, particularly those found in small streams, never grow larger than a few inches and are, therefore, not sought by fishermen. Others, such as the gizzard shad, which are bony or unpalatable, are called trash fish. All these fish, no matter how insignificant they may seem, are of interest when one considers their importance to each other and to the total aquatic system. The gizzard shad is probably the single most important source of food for adult largemouth bass and many other large predatory fish.

The rockfish or striped bass, a large cousin of the local white bass, is a saltwater species that can live and reproduce in some lakes and reservoirs in the southeastern states. Through a cooperative program between the states of Kentucky and Tennessee and TVA, this species has been stocked in both Kentucky Lake and Lake Barkley. The long-range success of the stocking program is yet to be determined.

The wealth of plant and animal life makes it possible for Land Between the Lakes to serve a wide range of recreational and educational interests including, fishing, birdwatching, photography, wildlife observation, nature study, and other outdoor activities. Wildlife photographers and birdwatchers are particularly attracted to the area in the early spring and fall when waterfowl and other migratory birds are most abundant. And the display of fall color that frames many of the trails and back-woods roads in Land Between the Lakes is one of the most spectacular in mid-America.

Two annual midwinter bird counts, including an eagle count in February, provide birdwatchers with an opportunity to get together and enjoy the outdoors during the quiet winter season. One of the most interesting and rewarding times to study wildlife in the Land Between the Lakes is after a light snowfall, when the habits and behavior patterns of animals can be studied by following their tracks as they search for food and shelter.

Hunting is allowed and welcomed throughout most of Land Between the Lakes on a managed basis. Although there is a wide variety of hunting in the area, the type and amount of hunting are subject to the dictates of sound wildlife management principles, and the seasons and species hunted may vary from year to year. Wild turkey, deer, squirrels, rabbits, raccoons, opossums, quail, doves, and waterfowl are presently hunted in Land Between the Lakes. Other animals such as beaver, bobcats, and woodchucks are on the protected list.

One of the most exciting hunting seasons in Land Between the Lakes is the spring hunt for wild turkey gobblers (hens are protected) that annually attracts hunters from all over the Midwest. Most hunters scout the area at daybreak for several days prior to the hunt in an effort to pinpoint locations of the "big toms" by listening for their gobble.

There are two deer hunting seasons held during the fall in Land Between the Lakes: a gun hunt and a bow hunt. During the gun hunt, a portion of the area is set aside for hunters who use pioneer weapons, and it is not unusual to see many of the muzzle-loading buffs stalking their prey in buckskins and coonskin caps. The bow season for deer attracts bow hunting clubs from a wide area. Many bow hunters consider the wide, palm-shaped rack of the fallow buck as one of the prize hunting trophies in the country. Both white-tailed and fallow deer are legal game in Land Between the Lakes.

Squirrel hunting probably provides more hours of hunting enjoyment than any other species in Land Between the Lakes. The oak-hickory type forest is an ideal habitat for the hardy gray and fox squirrels that thrive in the area, and they have universal appeal for hunters of all ages. The squirrel season usually begins in mid-August. Quail and rabbits are popular winter targets for small game hunters, and the big Canada geese along the shorelines of Kentucky Lake and Lake Barkley offer challenging sport for waterfowl hunters.

The length of hunting seasons, bag limits, and type of weapons used in Land Between the Lakes are consistent with state regulations, and a state hunting license is required to hunt game in the area.

Fishing is the favorite recreational pursuit of thousands of vacationers and sportsmen who visit Land Between the Lakes. The area is almost surrounded by two of the world's largest man-made lakes that offer excellent fishing for largemouth bass, crappie, white (stripe) bass, sauger, bluegill, and channel and blue catfish. Kentucky Lake, largest of TVA impoundments, has one of the largest annual harvests of panfish in the country. Each year, usually in April and May, tons of big, slab-sized crappie are caught when the fish move into the shallow bays and coves to spawn. Although the spring months produce the best crappie fishing, good catches are made throughout the year in deep water near the submerged river and creek channel banks.

The narrow bays and inlets and submerged brush in Lake Barkley make an ideal habitat for big largemouth bass, and limit strings of three- and four-pound bass are not uncommon. March through mid-June and September through November usually are the best periods for bass plugging in both Lake Barkley and Kentucky Lake. During the warm summer months many fishermen enjoy fishing for white bass —or "stripes"—when they are feeding on small bait fish near the surface (jump fishing). Night fishing for white bass under lantern light along the steep rock bluffs or around bridge abutments is also popular in July and August. Catfish are caught throughout the year below Barkley and Kentucky dams.

In addition to the three hundred miles of shoreline along Kentucky Lake and Lake Barkley, there are three subimpoundments on Lake Barkley, a small internal lake, and numerous ponds scattered throughout Land Between the Lakes. These bodies of water provide good fishing and are particularly popular with fishermen who prefer calm water.

The basic question to which the Land Between the Lakes demonstration is addressed is whether the manifold recreation and educational activities can be maintained under the impact of use generated by millions of visitors each year. To do so the plant and animal community on which they are based must be continually sustained and renewed. The visitor must be prepared to enter Land Between the Lakes as a member of this community—participating in the sustaining and renewal process.

Concern for the welfare of the total community must be the consuming responsibility of the area's administrators. This includes first the welfare of people, but further a recognition and understanding that the long-range welfare of people depends on the welfare of the total community environment.

In Land Between the Lakes one must start from the basic knowledge that the present natural community of soil, water, plants, and animals has been disturbed by man's past husbandry—or lack of it. Soil and forests are ailing. Numbers of wildlife are far below the capacity of the community to support. Man's exploitive and commodity-oriented economy here has failed and in its failure has impoverished the resource. So the first concern of the administrator must be to restore the basic health and prosperity of the community for its new role of public recreation.

While the new role requires a new set of goals and new patterns of land use, specific techniques may be no different from the old. The visitor should not be surprised, therefore, to see fields being mowed, crops being planted and harvested, or timber being cut. He need not be alarmed that the old, exploitive practices are being continued. Cropping and logging, as practiced in Land Between the Lakes, are efficient tools for restoring and maintaining a healthy balance and attractive environment for the sustenance of wildlife and the leisure of man.

Some of the practices, particularly logging, bushhogging, and bull-dozing, may involve immediate and short-term sacrifice of aesthetic values. They may even temporarily favor some species of wildlife or some of man's activities over others. But none is undertaken that does not promise long-range benefits to the overall health and welfare of the Land Between the Lakes community.

There will still be those with honest doubts that these measures, however well intentioned, can restore and sustain the resources of Land Between the Lakes for their intended purpose. The mere thought of visitors in the millions each year conjures up nightmares of trampled soil, dying trees, and vanishing wildlife. Those who continue to doubt may take comfort from the experience of European forests that comfortably sustain hundreds of times more visits each year than the most intensively used of American reserves. They do so because their managers have provided ample footpaths and people have learned to use them without littering or trampling adjacent vegetation. Manager, user, and resource are members of a single community drawing on each other for mutual support.

The goal of the Land Between the Lakes demonstration thus becomes a wisely planned collaboration between man and nature. Through conservation education a better balance between man and nature can become the goal of all public recreation areas in the United States.

Chapter Twelve

Into the Future

FLEXIBILITY to meet changing needs will continue to be the major hallmark of TVA's plans for the continued development of Land Between the Lakes. Plans to accommodate an increasing number of campers and day visitors have been prepared in varying degrees of completeness and will be put into effect as funds become available. These represent the most pressing need in terms of immediate service to the public to alleviate the present conditions where thousands of visitors may have to be turned away throughout the vacation months. But even the most rudimentary of these facilities will be modified to offer improvements that become clear through the experience of current operation, or which this same experience indicates as worthy of experimentation in the effort to offer the most practicable broad range of outdoor exposure for the visitor.

The most imaginative plan changes are likely to develop from operation of the Conservation Education Center. The early practicable experience in operating the Youth Center has strengthened TVA's early concept that conservation education programs should be primarily concerned with young people, and with the greatest emphasis for those of elementary school level. To keep the emphasis on children, a center for adult conservation programs will be relatively isolated, although adjacent to the other conservation center facilities. New emphasis will be placed throughout Land Between the Lakes on family-oriented conservation exhibits and activities, with the idea that the overall family exposure will be of help in providing a lasting impression upon the children.

Instead of a detailed blueprint to be followed rigidly, the Land Between the Lakes development program is primarily one of broad outlines. A recreation pattern restricted to the needs and concepts of

1970 would certainly have lost much of its relevancy by the year 2000, and likely even by 1980. Flexibility will provide a lasting value to TVA's valuable contribution to the whole Land Between the Lakes development—the opportunity to demonstrate new ideas and new patterns without rigid conformity to past procedures in the recreation and outdoor utilization field.

Although student visitor programs to the Conservation Education Center are expected to continue to be a major activity, there is no thought of attempting to offer these programs to all the available school population within the adjacent states. The immediate reason is that there would not be enough space or facilities, but the most important one is that the demonstration has already begun to achieve the desired result in public schools and other public agencies which work with young people—they are establishing their own conservation education programs and facilities close to home, but using the same basic methods demonstrated at Land Between the Lakes.

Paducah, Kentucky, is the nearest example of a school system that adopted its own conservation education program from the Land Between the Lakes demonstration, but DeKalb County, Georgia, 500 miles away, has made full use of Land Between the Lakes in its training program for teachers.

The interest at the high school and elementary student levels in the first national observance of "Earth Day" on April 22, 1970, is the best evidence of the need for an expanding conservation theme in general schoolwork. Achieving a balance of nature with the needs and survival of man will be too incomprehensible a theme for either children or adults without an increased and knowledgeable exposure to nature.

For schools throughout the country, new courses in environmental and ecological education (already being labeled EEE) are likely to become the most important curriculum change of the 1970s. Environmental education will, of course, be more than mere observance of nature, but appreciation of the entire ecological balance sheet should be an essential part of environmental programs for the classroom. The best motivation for an individual learning how best to protect the environment from destruction is full comprehension of nature in an outdoor exposure. The chlorophyll of a spreading leaf is more comprehensible in the woods, and the actualities of pollination are more evident when accompanied by the buzz of hungry bees. The chance to see ducks nesting along the lakeside where tadpoles swarm amidst the debris of winter is still the best introduction to the ecological cycle. Those school systems which have already begun to make use of the Conservation Education Center, and its related activities, will be well ahead toward the establishment of a balanced EEE curriculum.

The necessity for planned reservation and acquisition of open space lands as an adjunct to educational policy is another evidence that projections of the 1960s are already outdated. Population growth in the United States may not proceed at the high rate that has been predicted, but even a lesser population with enough concern for the environment to accept fewer of the value-destroying trappings of affluence is going to demand a greater access to open land. The urgency for open space will demand any type of land, not necessarily that with strong scenic or historic values. The environment of the future will not be likely to put a large share of our people into a sustaining contact with the natural world, but it should at least give the great majority of that population an opportunity to seek that contact occasionally.

Land Between the Lakes is located in a relatively isolated part of the central United States, and the actual land between the rivers probably changed less in the hundred years prior to the coming of the TVA program than it did in the first fifty years of white settlement. Despite the special condition of this relatively small tract, however, the overall region of western Kentucky and Tennessee witnessed the same changing patterns as did all the Southeast. The dominant characteristic of this change has perhaps been the fading of independent living and working conditions based on the old agrarian economy of the traditional South and Midwest. This has been followed by the emergence of a far more complex pattern of urban living based on an industrialized economy. The many streams of economic and social life, once looked upon as separate and self-sufficient, have reached an interdependence which can be very stimulating to concepts of the future. It can also be very depressing if people, in the process, are further removed from exposure to nature and natural elements.

The newly affluent people of our industrial society still seek out nature. In California, where the sheer magnitude of development has produced perhaps the greatest reaction against some of its sprawling and unlovely by-products, is one of the major examples of the inevitable confrontations between park and public which are developing as open space comes at a higher and higher premium in our country. Yosemite National Park, from the start one of the great prizes of our park system, simply cannot accommodate many thousands of the would-be visitors, primarily campers, and is approaching the point of having to turn away many of the motorists who want to drive through the park. The question is arising as to whether the park can be saved from the people.

Yosemite, like Yellowstone and the other great mountain parks of the West, was developed as much as a tourist attraction as for any other purpose, as a study of its history reveals. In the day when travel to the relatively remote sites of the parks meant only affluent tourists or the most hardy breed of adventurous hikers, there was little problem with crowds. Money—or the lack of it—and isolation preserved the park for those fortunate enough to be able to visit it.

John Muir, the pioneer California conservationist, said of the Yosemite country: "Climb the mountains and get their good tidings. Nature's peace will flow into you as sunshine flows into trees. The winds will blow their own freshness into you and the storms their energy, while cares will drop off like the autumn leaves." But there is no room for all the tourists who come in response to Muir's invitation. Each night in the summer many who come without reservations for either lodge or campsite have to spend the night in their cars. Each new plan for enlarging the hotel and lodge facilities, or adding more campsites, brings enraged protests from disciples of Muir, who complain about hikers ruining the trails and leaving Yosemite scarred and marred. The national parks, established as "pleasuring grounds for the people," obviously have too many people. Yet no rational policy of a democratic government would bar the people from the beauties of nature which have been specifically set aside for preservation. The only answer can be more open space set aside and carefully administered for public recreation, and conservation education where the public is willing to accept it.

Land Between the Lakes has been established as a demonstration of the direction national policy can go in attempting to meet this need. Its experience in acquiring land demonstrates the value and effectiveness of a carefully planned, stable program as the only way of obviating difficulties which are bound to develop, even under the most favorable circumstances.

The visitors to Land Between the Lakes already have included large numbers from every part of the country, but obviously the largest part of those served will continue to be from within a 500-mile radius of the area, primarily from mid-America. This will mean several million visitations annually and in itself will be a valid reason for the existence of Land Between the Lakes, because most of these visitors will be from areas where there are no comparable federal recreation areas.

Its role as a demonstration for other publicly supported conservation-based recreation areas should continue to be its most important function, however. The impact it will have on the planning, establishment, and operation of other outdoor recreation and conservation education centers elsewhere in the country should help to eliminate many hesitant and wasteful steps along the way. Providing adequate open-space recreation for our country before the turn of the century is going to be costly enough, without having to pursue false leads and undeveloped ideas, to say nothing of the added costs and frustrations of stop-and-go development, all too much of the limited pattern of the past.

Land Between the Lakes will not be a successful demonstration if it becomes a static institution, with repetitive conventional campgrounds and other facilities and services which offer no basic difference, improvement, or innovation from those which were built yesterday or are being built elsewhere today. The same eclectic, experimental approach that was the hallmark of its planning must apply to its continuing program.

The very nature of the demonstration precludes any exact time span being established for its duration. Perhaps some still undefined development in the overall field in the future will preclude the relevance or value as a continuing demonstration. Until that development becomes clear, however, Land Between the Lakes can help define for all the country the kind of action which must be taken if our natural heritage is to remain accessible to the people.

Index

[With the exception of one alphabetic listing each, Land Between the Lakes will be designated as LBL and National Park Service as NPS]